Empowering Bystanders In Bullying Prevention

D0664701

Grades K-8 • Stan Davis with Julia Davis

Research Press ○ 2612 North Mattis Avenue ○ Champaign, Illinois 61822 ○ (800) 519-2707

www.researchpress.com

Copies of this book may be ordered from Research Press at the address given on the title page.

Composition by Jeff Helgesen
Cover design by Linda Brown, Positive I.D. Graphic Design, Inc.
Printed by Malloy, Inc.

ISBN-13: 978–0-87822-539–2
ISBN-10: 0–87822-539–0
Library of Congress Control Number 2007928220

Contents

Acknowledgments

To the staff and students at the James H. Bean Elementary School in Sidney, Maine, who demonstrate the power of caring and connection every day

To the many researchers and practitioners who have generously shared their research, advice, and critical feedback, with special thanks to Marlene Snyder, Lyn Mikel Brown, and Steve Danish

Most of all, thanks to Ron Zorn, who taught me to pay attention to the details

Introduction

Bystanders who are helpless in the presence of another student's victimization learn passive acceptance of injustice.

—Jeffrey, Miller, and Linn (2001, p. 145)

Injustice anywhere is a threat to justice everywhere.

—Martin Luther King Jr.

When children learn to accept exclusion and cruelty and see themselves as incapable of creating change, they learn a lifelong lesson: passive acceptance of injustice. In many ways, we live within a culture that continues to accept injustice. The United States has a history of oppression, unequal power dynamics, and aggression toward marginalized populations. While it is true that much has improved since the civil rights and women's suffrage movements, prejudice and discrimination remain common, and children often learn to accept injustice both through their experiences in school and as members of a wider community. Our country—and the world as a whole—needs active citizens who work for justice.

In 2006, school staff and I surveyed 1,409 kindergarten through 12th graders at a school system in Massachusetts. I asked them to choose one of two options to complete the following statement: "When I see someone being teased or hit, I think . . ." Their options were "They deserve it" or "They don't deserve it." As shown in the graph on the next page, I found older students more likely than younger students to state that targets of bullying deserve to be hit or teased. This finding points strongly to a learned acceptance of bullying behavior.

I have worked as an activist for social justice for causes including civil rights, peace, and prevention of domestic abuse

1

Percentage

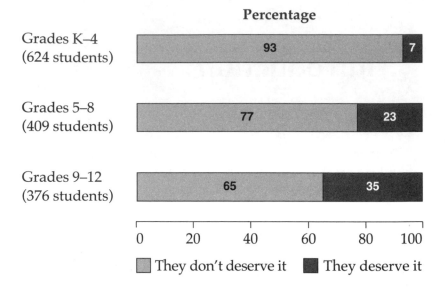

Grades K–4
(624 students)

Grades 5–8
(409 students)

Grades 9–12
(376 students)

☐ They don't deserve it   ■ They deserve it

and rape. When I began to understand the broad implications of school bullying, I embarked on a campaign for social justice in my current subset of the larger culture—the elementary school where I continue to work. During my 20 years as a school guidance counselor, I have observed abuse of power, inequality, intolerance, and exclusion. I have also seen young people act on strong feelings of altruism and idealism. The challenge for us as adults, who naturally possess a great deal of influence over the culture of schools, is to help students maintain their natural idealism and empathy while learning effective skills to act in the face of injustice. We have the power to "think globally—act locally," one school at a time. Students at the James H. Bean Elementary School in Sidney, Maine, where my colleagues and I developed and tested most of the interventions described in this book, chose a new school slogan in the fall of 2006: "The James H. Bean School: With kindness and fairness for all." With respect and admiration for the work our staff and students have done, I can proudly say that this slogan accurately reflects our school's culture.

In 1998, we implemented a bullying prevention program based largely on the research of Dr. Dan Olweus (1993, 2001). Over the years, we have fine-tuned and added to the program and have seen dramatic and continuing reductions in student reports of bullying. For example, from the 1998–1999 school year to the 2006–2007 school year, our fifth graders reported a 95 percent reduction in physical bullying, a 92 percent reduction in teasing, and a 96 percent reduction in exclusion. Detailed survey data from the Bean school and a detailed description of the program can be found at www.stopbullyingnow.com/beandata.pdf.

I wrote my first book, *Schools Where Everyone Belongs: Practical Strategies for Reducing Bullying,* over a period of four years. Published in 2005 by Research Press, this book describes the essential foundations of bullying prevention programs and documents techniques for building consistent and effective school discipline systems, connecting staff with students, and helping aggressive youth change their behavior. This second book briefly reviews these foundations before discussing interventions that build on them, especially as they relate to empowering bystanders in bullying situations.

I chose to write a second book for several reasons. For the past eight years, I have trained school staff across the United States and Canada in effective techniques to reduce bullying. Over time, my trainings have evolved as a result of new research, questions I receive from educators, and my work at the Bean school. One of the most common questions trainees ask me since *Schools Where Everyone Belongs* was published is how to lead effective classroom discussions about bullying. This book is, in part, an answer to these questions.

Also since the first book's publication, the bullying prevention program at the Bean school has evolved. Now in its ninth year, the program has grown from a staff-led intervention to a partnership between students and staff. Students at the Bean school have taken ownership of the program and now initiate their own interventions, with little adult-imposed structure. They work to improve school climate, design mentoring programs for younger students, find ways to reach out to isolated peers, and infuse school slogans with real meaning.

When reflecting on the success of our bullying prevention program, I believe it is the shared language, skills, and positive social norms that make the Bean school what it is today. As a result of our work toward these ends, we effectively stop bullying early on by limiting the rewards of bullying behavior and empowering the empathetic majority to fulfill their positive potential as active bystanders.

After school staff implement protective systems and build staff-student connections, they can deepen bullying prevention work by empowering bystanders of bullying, teaching social problem solving skills, and helping students create a positive and inclusive peer culture. Most students in any given school do not bully others; neither are they bullied. Students who see hitting, name-calling, and exclusion often feel deeply sympathetic toward targets and possess the potential to take effective action against bullying. Like community members in Neighborhood Watch programs, bystanders' collaborative efforts can have significant positive effects on school culture.

This book presents an approach to bullying prevention and student empowerment that is both research-based and practical. Research on the dynamics of change, learning styles, and the effectiveness or ineffectiveness of specific intervention techniques should inform our work. As James Garbarino often says in his workshops, "A wise person once said, 'You can change the world. But unless you know what you are doing . . . please don't!' " (personal communication, November 11, 2006). This book is also based on my 20 years' experience as a counselor in public schools at all grade levels, I am intimately acquainted with the inherent difficulties in and limitations on implementing bullying prevention interventions in a school environment. I hope this book's balance of research and practicality can provide school staff with the knowledge, skills, and sense of self-efficacy to create change in their own schools.

CONTENT OVERVIEW

This book is organized around alternating discussions of theory and practice. Chapter 1 discusses the importance of focusing on bystanders and the inherent difficulties of speaking out against bullying. I use parallels to adult life to outline some of the ideological shifts essential to effective bullying prevention in schools.

In chapter 2, I describe the foundations of bullying prevention programs. Before we can conduct student conversations around bystander empowerment and social norms, school staff should implement interventions to ensure the physical and emotional safety of all students. Described in depth in my first book, these interventions include staff-student connections and mentoring, consistent schoolwide discipline procedures focused on helping aggressive youth change, and support for targets of bullying.

Chapter 3 outlines techniques for helping young people build empathy and skills for social problem solving. Empathy, or the ability to understand and feel others' emotions, is an essential and teachable skill. When students develop a wide range of solutions to social problems, they become better able to choose solutions that work for them in each situation. When students possess skills and feel safe enough to use them, they can avoid and defuse many problems with peers.

In chapter 4, I describe in detail a student workshop focused on shifting attitudes and teaching skills necessary to empower bystanders to take effective action against bullying.

Chapter 5 focuses on the topic of developing shared language, social norms, and positive school culture—all of which have the power to shape how individuals and groups think and behave. Instead of passively accepting existing language and norms and the culture they create, we can work actively to recognize and change norms and language to align them with the messages of our bullying prevention program. This process can be initiated and driven by both staff and students.

Chapter 6 outlines two climate-based interventions implemented at the Bean school: student-created legacy videos and Peace Day assemblies. These two concrete examples show how to implement the interventions discussed in chapter 5. Chapter 6 is followed by a brief afterword describing what kinds of adult citizens can emerge from bullying prevention programs in schools.

Following these chapters, I include several appendixes to illustrate ways school staff and other professionals may apply chapter topics.

The scope and sequence of the guidance program we follow at the Bean school are the focus of Appendix A. This series of lessons and discussions helps students develop skills for interpersonal relationships. We start by teaching the youngest students to accept not always getting their way and manage their state of arousal. We work with students in the middle grades to develop social problem solving skills and techniques for bystander action. We strive to empower the oldest students to design and implement initiatives to create a safe and inclusive peer culture.

Appendix B consists of a detailed lesson plan for using Eleanor Estes's 1988 book *The Hundred Dresses* (2004/1944) as a tool to increase motivation, knowledge, and skills in bystander situations. I have found this book to be extremely helpful in my teaching, but school staff could apply the same type of analysis and teaching techniques to other books as well.

Appendix C outlines a lesson plan focusing on relational aggression called "First, Do No Harm." This and similar lessons teach young people to avoid being pulled into conflicts between friends in ways that make those conflicts worse. Instead, we can help young people use positive solutions when they observe friendship conflicts.

"Recess School," the subject of Appendix D, is a program instituted at the Bean school to teach young students skills to play peacefully and reduce playground aggression.

Appendix E describes lessons focusing on a radio broadcast of the program *This American Life* titled "Shouting across the Divide" (Glass, 2006). This true story about a Muslim student's experiences can help students better understand issues of diversity and encourage bystander action. The program is available for download or purchase at www.thisamericanlife.org.

The use of magic effects to shift student attitudes toward bullying, inclusion, and social justice is the topic of Appendix F.

Finally, in Appendix G, my daughter and co-author, Julia, adds depth to the discussion by describing the connections between the ideas in this book and the goals and methods in her work at Summit Achievement, a wilderness-based therapeutic program for teens.

The strategies presented in this book are the result of almost 40 years' work as a therapist and counselor. They are the result of many successes, but also of many failures and mistakes. They have evolved over time and continue to evolve according to what works for me and for a particular group of students in a particular school setting. I write about interventions in great detail because training audiences consistently ask for these details. In doing so, I attempt to provide for readers the experience of an observer. Rather than expecting you to copy the questions and actions I provide, I encourage you to use these examples to create your own interventions. Please adapt the lessons and techniques described in this book to fit your own style and students' needs. The interventions will be most effective when you take them on as your own, pick and choose the best for your situation, and modify them to fit your needs.

This book is organized differently than *Schools Where Everyone Belongs*. *Schools* is a summary of research and a detailed handbook for step-by-step implementation of bullying prevention programs. This book is more like a cookbook, mixing fundamental principles, practical and tested techniques, and detailed specific recipes. As with any cookbook, please feel free to adapt the techniques to your own situation and style. As with any recipe, please change the details to suit the ingredients you have at hand, the inspiration of the moment, and your own taste. I look forward to your reactions, questions, discoveries, and additions. You can reach me via e-mail at stan@stopbullyingnow.com.

Chapter 1

Empowering Bystanders of Bullying

In the end we will remember not the words of our enemies, but the silence of our friends.

—Martin Luther King Jr.

When I began talking with young people about bullying, I followed the lead of most of the videos on the market and the other speakers I could find. I addressed the bullies in the audience, trying to convince them that name-calling and exclusion hurt. I quickly became aware that those students were not listening to me. They might clown around or disrupt my presentations. They might, instead, act as though they were very concerned. A teacher stopped me from focusing on bullies by writing on a feedback form: "Great presentation. Too bad the students who needed it weren't listening." For reasons described elsewhere in this book, I do not believe we should focus student discussions primarily on what targets of bullying should do to avoid being bullied. Many of these students already feel that they deserve the torment they are receiving; telling them to change their behavior to stop the bullying risks reinforcing that self-blame. I learned that peer bystanders, who represent the vast majority of any student body, have the willingness and the potential power to make a dramatic difference.

WHY FOCUS ON BYSTANDERS?

As I see it, there are three reasons that focusing on fostering awareness, empathy, and action in bystanders is an essential element of bullying prevention programs.

Bystanders Can Provide Crucial Support for Youth Who Are Bullied

Young people who are bullied often perceive the silence and inaction of their peers as an indication that everyone thinks they deserve to be treated poorly. This belief often leads targets to blame themselves for the bullying they experience. One middle school student said: "First they bully you—then you bully yourself." A high school student wrote to me: "If no one does anything and the bullying goes on long enough, you start believing that what they say about you is true." When targets of any form of abuse or harassment blame themselves, they are more likely to experience long-term emotional damage.

In addition, young people who are bullied often become socially isolated, which can have serious effects on their emotional development and may inhibit their ability to develop essential skills for building and maintaining friendships. Nansel, Overpeck, Pilla, Ruan, Simons-Morton, and Scheidt (2001) found that students who were bullied reported higher rates of loneliness, more trouble making friends, and poorer relationships with classmates. We need go no further to understand the emotional impact of this loneliness than to look into the tear-filled eyes of the fifth-grade boy who handed me a piece of paper with the words "I hate my life" scrawled on it. He later told me that his best friend now plays with other people and he has no friends in his grade. For preteens and teenagers especially, having no friends is an intensely painful experience. Before I developed the techniques for assisting isolated students in building friendships described in chapter 5 of this book, I saw few ways to help besides offering my own friendship to isolated youth. Their responses always included polite thanks with a reminder that what I was offering was not what they needed. "It's not the same thing," said one student. Adult friends don't play with students at recess, invite them to birthday parties, sit with them at lunch, or choose them for group work in class.

Peer bystanders, more than adults, are in a unique situation to send targets the crucial messages that those who choose to bully are responsible for their actions and that targets are not to blame. This cognitive shift helps reduce the damage done to targets of bullying.

Empathetic and active peer bystanders can fill a vital friendship role by inviting isolated students to sit with them, play with them, join games and activities, and be seen with them. Sometimes this leads to friendship between bystanders and isolated youth. Other times, simply being seen with high-status peers leads others to reach out to isolated youth.

Bystanders Can Provide Support for Youth Who Bully Others

Research by Olweus (1993, 2001) and Juvonen, Graham, and Schuster (2003), among many others, differentiates young people who bully into two categories: bully-victims, who often have low social status and few positive peer connections, and high-status bullies, who often have considerable peer support and high social status. For each of these groups, bystander behavior can have a significant positive impact. Bully-victims benefit when well-behaved, well-respected peers are willing to connect with them in helping ways. I believe Hekter, August, & Realmuto (2003) were referring to these students in their article "Effects of Pairing Aggressive and Nonaggressive Children in Strategic Peer Affiliation," when they wrote:

> Moderately disruptive boys did appear to be susceptible to peer influence. Those with aggressive friends became more delinquent, whereas those with nonaggressive friends were rated at 13 as less delinquent. (p. 399)

Hekter et al. also address people's concerns about the effects of these mentoring relationships on nonaggressive youth:

> Moderately or highly conforming boys with aggressive friends at age 11 or 12 were no more delinquent at age 13 than those with average or nonaggressive friends. These nondeviant boys did not appear to have been influenced by their more aggressive friends. (p. 399)

From my own experience, I have seen the power of positive peer connections to help aggressive youth change. Recently, I ran a lunchtime friendship skills group for some of our isolated fourth graders who were driving peers away by engaging in provocative and aggressive behaviors. Partway through the year, a few of our well-liked students asked if they could join this lunchtime group. After joining the group, these concerned peers quickly began to watch for the group members' positive behavior changes in the classroom and other settings. They would then excitedly report back to the whole group about group members' prosocial actions. This specific positive feedback from well-accepted peers was clearly deeply moving for formerly excluded and aggressive youth, and consistently led to stable behavior change.

High-status bullies benefit when peer bystanders consciously withdraw social reinforcement for aggressive, excluding, or harassing behavior. For two years in succession, Bean school fifth graders stopped the development of a powerful, popular group. In each case, a small group of well-respected students tried to achieve power over others through threats to withdraw friendship, party invitations, and group membership from students who would not do what they said. In each case, other students brought their concerns about this trend to school staff and decided to calmly refuse to accept the demands and manipulations of this self-labeled popular group. The students who tried to create a popular group thus received no power or other reinforcement for their efforts, and they soon stopped trying to gain power in this way. As Lord Acton said in 1887, "Power tends to corrupt."

Action or Inaction Affects Bystanders

Richard Hazler summarizes the article "Trauma Reactions of Bystanders and Victims to Repetitive Abuse Experiences": "Children and adult bystanders who witness repeated abuse inflicted on others may experience both a psychological and physiological stress level that, over time, can equal that of the victim"(Janson & Hazler, 2004, para. 1). Ellen DeLara quotes a young man as saying: "Yeah, I see kids get bullied every day at my school. Nobody stops it. It makes you feel kind of bad inside. You can feel it in your stomach" (Garbarino & DeLara, 2002, p. xiii). Our own life experiences confirm these words. At some point in our lives, most of us have witnessed bullying or abusive behaviors and have felt helpless to remedy the situation. All of us who have been in this situation understand the depth and lasting nature of the guilt arising from our own inaction.

Every time bystanders act effectively to stop bullying, they see their own potential to make a positive impact on the world. This feeling of being capable, even in the face of challenge, can enrich their lives and lead them to continue to act positively and effectively.

The most powerful experience of my life arose from this same feeling of being capable of enacting positive change in a flawed world. Two months before my 18th birthday, I traveled south from Boston with a group to join more than 20,000 bystanders from every part of the United States for the final leg of the 1965 voting rights march from Selma to Montgomery, Alabama. Civil rights leaders had appealed for support after attacks on a smaller march left protesters beaten and bleeding by the roadside. The organizers of the march sought strength in numbers, and tens of thousands of Americans responded to their plea for help. The successful completion of the voting rights march, and the widespread support shown to protesters, led to the passage and signing of the U.S. Voting Rights Act shortly afterward. While many of my memories are now hazy, one moment remains crystal clear in my mind. I remember marching across the Edmund Pettis Bridge, between Selma and Montgomery, to the sounds of jeering and threats from segregationists. In reply, someone in the crowd of marchers started singing the song, "Ain't Gonna Let Nobody Turn Me 'Round." I found myself singing and marching in perfect unison with thousands of people who shared a passionate vision of justice and human progress. In that moment, my fear lifted and I was filled with a light that has never left me. That light has sustained and supported me in my life's work. There is no experience so profoundly transforming as working with others to stop injustice and prevent the suffering of others.

DIFFICULTIES BYSTANDERS FACE: THREE EXAMPLES

One day in February, I was walking down a hallway in the Bean school about an hour after our students had left for home. From around the corner I heard a girl yelling, "Ow!" and I sped up to turn the corner. I saw a boy in his early teens holding a slightly younger girl in a wrestling hold. His arms were threaded under her armpits, and his hands were cupped over the back of her neck, pressing her head forward. She was yelling in pain. From where I stood I yelled, "Cut it out!" He turned to me without releasing his grip and said, "It's okay. She's my sister." I told him again to stop. He released his grip and said to me, "You can't tell me what to do. You're not my father." I realized that these two teens were probably in the school for an extracurricular basketball game. I briefly looked around for their parents, though there were no other adults in the hallway. While I looked around, the girl returned to the gym. Soon I continued on my way.

In 1999, I attended an acting training workshop with a select group of professional magicians from all over the United States and Canada. I was in awe of some of the people attending this training and desperately wanted these accomplished professionals to accept and respect me. During the second day of the training, some of the men in the group began joking about a well-known stage magician who had recently been convicted of child sexual abuse and sent to jail. One of them said, "I'm not gay like him." Another one replied, "Yeah. That f***ing queer." I was horrified, yet conflicted. The misconception that child molesters are gay is common and naturally leads to homophobia, discrimination, and violence. I felt uncomfortable quietly accepting bigotry and indirect harassment. I felt equally uncomfortable rebuking these men and risking rejection. After a few minutes' thought, I took a deep breath and said, "The way I understand it, some people are attracted to the opposite sex, some are attracted to the same sex, and some are attracted to children. Being a pedophile has nothing to do with being straight or gay, and because the odds are that at least one of the 15 of us is gay, I am uncomfortable with that kind of talk." I held my breath to see what would happen next. Nobody looked at me for a minute, but then they went back to talking about other magicians they knew. The magicians accepted and respected me throughout the rest of the workshop, and there were no further homophobic comments made in my presence.

In the spring of 2006, I was sitting at a bus stop in a rough neighborhood in a large, unfamiliar city far from my home. It was late at night. Two other adults, whom I did not know, also waited at the bus stop. Five large, muscular teenagers appeared, yelling and pushing each other in rough good spirits. Suddenly, four of them grabbed the fifth, bent him over, pushed his head to the sidewalk, and simulated having sex with him. Their intent was clearly to humiliate him. He lunged free and, with a mixture of rage and embarrassment in his voice, yelled for them to stop. He tried to hit them while they laughed, danced out of his way, pulled him off each other, and made his anger into a game. The other two adults and I averted our eyes. I was sure that I should do something but found myself rooted to the spot. I thought about my options. I could approach these tough teenagers, each almost as big as myself, and tell them to stop. I imagined that they might throw me to the ground and beat me up. I could approach the target. Even if I could figure out something to say to him, he was so angry it seemed likely that he might attack me as well. I could call for help or try to find a police officer, but I didn't know where to find a police officer and wasn't sure if the police would care or respond in time to address the problem. I imagined that attempting to contact authorities might lead the teens to assault me when an officer did not arrive. What I did was the same as the other two adults at the bus stop: We waited for our buses and gratefully boarded when they arrived. I rode away on the bus guiltily, deeply saddened by my inability to remedy the situation.

Being an active bystander is rarely as easy for peers as it is for adult authority figures in schools. Bystanders' ability or inability to intervene effectively in bullying situations depends on many factors, and no two bystander scenarios are the same. Four of the primary factors illustrated in the previous three examples are power, safety (including access to backup), social acceptance, and knowledge of effective interventions.

Power

Power may arise from being in a position of authority (e.g., school staff) or from a difference in age or strength between bystanders and aggressors. When bystanders possess more power than bullies, they are better able to intervene directly. The first scenario illustrates a power differential due to my greater age, size, and status. I ran little risk by intervening and had a good chance of being effective. It is important to remember that student bystanders *do not* possess this kind of power over youth who bully.

Safety

When bystanders lack power, they can still act if they feel safe and have access to proper backup. Safety comes from knowing that we can protect ourselves or that others will protect us if we act against bullying. In the last example, I felt unsafe. Lacking support and protection and being in an unfamiliar city left me helpless. I did not access backup in any of the examples described above. In the first two examples, I felt safe and had enough power to intervene on my own. In the third example, I did not see accessing backup (i.e., law enforcement) as being a practical or safe solution. I had no cell phone and did not know the location of the nearest police station. I also did not know if what I was seeing was actually reportable criminal behavior. On a deeper, emotional level, I was so horrified by what I saw that I was immobilized. When bystanders feel safe and encouraged to ask those with power for help, they can enlist others to make a difference.

Social Acceptance

There are two factors involved in social acceptance and rejection. First, the culture of a school or community helps determine the social pressures on individuals. In environments where speaking up against injustice is clearly accepted and valued, the risks of social rejection for active bystanders are reduced. In environments where youth who bully hold the power to determine acceptance or rejection, the risks of speaking up are greater. In addition, individuals vary in their willingness to risk social rejection. Every action entails a risk; therefore, decisions rely in part on our dedication to fighting for what we believe in. In the second example, despite the lack of a physical threat, I saw challenging the homophobic statement as risky. Looking back, I believe I spoke up because I found, as teenagers have told me, that confronting someone using hate speech not directed at a particular person is less threatening than interrupting direct verbal or physical harassment. I was willing to risk social rejection to follow my convictions. At the same time, it is important not to underestimate how difficult even this action can be. I was 50 years old in this example and thus less concerned about others' reactions to my behavior than I had been as a young person. I had already learned to speak my mind effectively during the civil rights movement, during conflicts between angry youth and their families in my therapy office, and while working to resolve community conflict as a school board chair, town selectman, and mental health center administrator. I had learned over time that while speaking up in these situations sometimes leads to short-term anger, long-term negative consequences are unlikely. For youth, the risk of speaking up against indirect harassment is more daunting than it is for adults. In chapter 5, I will discuss strategies to help encourage young people to intervene effectively when they hear indirect harassment. Adult modeling, shared positive social norms, and knowledge of the effects of bullying on targets help to determine how willing young people will be to risk social rejection.

Knowledge of Effective Actions

The last major factor in determining action or inaction in bystander situations is knowledge of effective actions. As shown in the three examples above, effective bystander actions vary for each individual and in each situation. It is essential for young people to master a range of safe and effective solutions. I will describe interventions focused on skill development in detail in chapter 3.

CHALLENGES IN EMPOWERING BYSTANDERS TO ACT

I describe and discuss the previous scenarios to underline the difficulty inherent in empowering bystanders to act. As adults in schools, especially elementary schools, we possess a great deal of power due to our size, age, and status as authority figures. We also have learned and practiced many skills and are willing to risk experiencing a certain amount of anger and rejection. Being accustomed to acting from this position of power and knowledge can lead us to forget that young people experience the world from a very different perspective. We should attempt to address these challenges and help young people access the knowledge, safety, backup, and personal motivation to make their bystander actions safe and effective. As Stueve, Dash, O'Donnell, Tehranifar, Wilson-Simmons, Slaby, and Link (2006) write:

> [Youth] are less likely to intervene if they believe that the costs of acting are excessive, believe that significant others would not intervene or expect them to do so, or perceive substantial barriers to acting effectively. . . . Bystanders are more likely to act if they know what to do and feel that they possess the necessary resources. (p. 120)

The first step, then, is to understand the challenges students face as bystanders and how adults make it harder or easier for them to make a difference.

CONFRONTATION AND OTHER SOLUTIONS

Advice for young bystanders of bullying abounds. Much of this advice focuses on, or at least begins with, direct confrontation. Years ago, I tried to help students develop nonviolent techniques to confront bullies. During my student workshops, I would enlist young people to play the roles of bully, target, and bystanders. When I asked the audience what the bystanders could do to help, the first answer was almost always to tell the bully to stop. When bystanders would demonstrate this strategy by yelling at the bully, I tried to help them develop nonviolent confrontation techniques. After practicing this solution, we brainstormed other possible interventions, such as helping the target get away, telling a teacher, or befriending the target later. Students throughout the United States and Canada repeatedly told me that confronting aggressive youth is what they should do. Yet as I have gotten to know these young people better during follow-up sessions, they have also told me that they don't confront peers who bully. This reluctance to confront peers is rooted primarily in concerns for their own safety and fear of losing friends.

When confrontation is on the table as a possible solution, students are less likely to remember or use other solutions. Their thought process focuses so much on confrontation that they forget about everything else we brainstorm and practice. When students don't feel safe confronting youth who bully but remain stuck in the mind-set that this is what they should do, they often give up—learning a powerful lesson of their own inefficacy.

A group of high school students further clarified the issue of direct confrontation for me when they asked me whether I confront adults who behave in ways I disagree with. They asked me what I do if I see a parent speaking abusively to a child in the supermarket or witness a robbery in progress. They asked me what I do when a colleague yells at or insults students at my school or when I disagree with the way my friends or relatives raise their children. Like most adults, I do not use confrontation in most of these situations for the same reasons as young people: fear of making the situation worse, fear for my own safety, and fear of losing friends.

Thus my own personal observations and young people's honesty have taught me that advising young people to confront bullies is unrealistic and ineffective. When we focus our conversations on bystander action around confrontation, we encourage students to see this as the only solution. As Jackson Katz writes in *The Macho Paradox*, a book that describes what men can do to prevent male violence toward women, "Many people mistakenly believe that they have only two options in instances of actual or potential violence: intervene physically and possibly expose themselves to personal harm, or do nothing" (2006, p. 214). When we discourage direct confrontation, people of all ages become free to learn, practice, and use a range of other effective and safe solutions.

THE NEIGHBORHOOD WATCH EXAMPLE

Another useful parallel that can shift our perceptions around what to teach student bystanders in schools comes from Neighborhood Watch programs. These programs empower local volunteers to make their communities safer by partnering with police. It makes sense that when we recruit and train bystanders to act against bullying, we should have goals similar to those of a Neighborhood Watch program: to inspire community involvement, encourage citizens to assist authority figures, and build a cohesive neighborhood culture.

Neighborhood Watch programs provide clear messages for their volunteers. They explicitly forbid volunteers from intervening directly when they see someone breaking the law. Instead, volunteers are encouraged to be the eyes and ears of the police and to support the victims of crimes. These tasks are crucial to effective law enforcement and inclusive, safe communities. The emphasis on protection of witnesses, practicality of encouraged interventions, strength in numbers, and community support help Neighborhood Watch programs be successful. Youth in schools can become effective bystanders of bullying as a result of similar interventions. Bystanders need protection from retaliation, skills for safe and effective interventions, and the belief that bystander action is an accepted and valued element in school culture.

Paying Attention and Reporting the Truth

In both community crime and bullying in schools, authorities often encounter difficulty ascertaining exactly what occurred during a reported incident. In schools, the alleged target and the alleged bully often give very different accounts of an incident. Peers often observe the behavior but adhere to a code of silence. When bystanders commit to paying attention and reporting the truth to adults, schools and communities become safer places. Targets of bullying are more likely to ask for help when they know witnesses will tell the truth. Youth who bully are more likely to change when they are held accountable for their behavior. We can even help young people who are friends with bullies see that when they tell adults about their friends' behaviors, they are helping the friends develop more positive behavior patterns and avoid getting in trouble later.

In both community and school situations, we should make it clear that witnesses may choose to report as little or as much as they feel comfortable with. Community members may inform the police anonymously that a particular parking lot has become a frequent location for late-night drug deals, and students may inform staff that aggression is common in a certain locker room or bathroom.

Challenging the Code of Silence

While it is clear that schools are safer for all when students communicate openly with adults and feel comfortable asking for help, the truth is that young people, especially in middle school, often adhere to a strong code of silence. Gaughan, Cerio, and Myers (2001) report the results of a Harris Poll survey, completed two years after the Columbine shootings, showing that only 54 percent of middle school and high school students surveyed said they would tell an adult if they heard another student talking about shooting someone at school. In explaining why students don't tell adults about violence in schools, Stueve et al. (2006) write:

> When asked why they failed to notify adults about incidents of violence, students listed a variety of reasons for maintaining their silence. They did not think the school assailants would act on their threats, were afraid of retribution, were concerned about the well-being of the aggressor or some other party, did not know where to go for assistance, doubted they would be believed, or did not think anything would be done if they reported what they knew. (p. 121)

Student silence is thus based on many factors. One is a deeply rooted aversion to "tattling," a topic I will discuss in detail in chapter 5. Youth who bully and their allies often threaten bystanders and targets with retaliation and exclusion. In order to encourage young people to tell adults about bullying, adults should establish the safety of those who tell by discarding the concept of tattling and doing everything in our power to prevent retaliation. For schools to become telling environments, we have to enact the same conceptual shifts that led us to see people who report a company dumping mercury into a river as whistleblowers, rather than rats. I talked with a group of middle school students in upstate New York about their fear of retaliation for telling adults about bullying. When asked why adults report crimes, they replied, "Adults must be braver than we are." These students were surprised when their school resource officer told them about laws that protect witnesses and informed them that retaliation against witnesses often brings more serious consequences than the initial crime. Peer bystanders need the same support if they are to tell us the truth. School staff must protect the confidentiality of young people and protect them from retaliation. We must take seriously and show appreciation for young people who report the truth. Without these interventions, the risks of telling may outweigh the benefits. Since telling adults about incidents of bullying is one of the primary ways bystanders can access power to make a difference, we should explicitly and implicitly address their concerns.

Creating a Supportive Environment

Another task of Neighborhood Watch volunteers and bystanders of bullying is to create a mutually supportive neighborhood culture. Community support is a crucial component of healing for victims of crime. Without this support, victims may begin to see the world as a dangerous, isolating place. This sense of danger and isolation can sometimes be more traumatic than the crime itself. Likewise, peer isolation can be the most traumatizing element of being bullied in school. Mynard, Joseph, and Alexander (2000) compared the effects of hitting, verbal victimization (name-calling), and social manipulation (systematic exclusion) on adolescents. They found that social manipulation by peers had the most severe negative effects and could result in symptoms of post-traumatic stress disorder. Blacher and Eisenhower write in "Overcoming Peer Rejection and Promoting Friendship":

> Children who are chronically rejected by their peers are more likely to suffer from internalizing disorders, problems such as depression, anxiety, loneliness, or low self-esteem. Children who are rejected often display more externalizing disorders as well, such as aggression or acting out. . . . As adolescents and adults, poorly accepted children are more likely to drop out of school, experience academic failure, demonstrate delinquent behavior, and develop psychiatric disorders. (2004, p. 1)

One of the most powerful actions that bystanders can take to help targets is to listen to them, invite them into activities, or sit and walk with them. Choosing to involve isolated peers can lead to friendship, which ultimately benefits both the bystander and the target. Over time, schools can become environments where it is seen as the job of all students to ensure that no one is excluded.

SUMMARY AND CONCLUSIONS

I began planning this book when I saw the need for school staff to shift away from a common set of assumptions in which "telling the bully to stop" is seen as the most courageous and valued bystander intervention. I argue for replacing this long-held belief with a more realistic, nuanced, and adaptable view of bystander action. To obtain this attitude shift, it is helpful to look beyond our experiences as inherently powerful school staff to our own experiences as powerless bystanders. As we begin to understand the difficulties of bystander action, we should remember not to give advice we are unwilling to follow in our own lives. As Eleanor Roosevelt said, "It is not fair to ask of others what you are unwilling to do yourself" (Lewis, n.d.). Whether or not young bystanders act when they observe bullying depends on adults' willingness to provide them with backup and assure their safety. We must help them reject risky or ineffective solutions and create a wide range of realistic, safe, and effective options for action. Their action or inaction also depends on adults' willingness to listen to and collaborate with young people over time to build a student culture in which peers reject the code of silence and value and actively work toward inclusion and justice. Peers' willingness to act depends on their ability to take responsibility for the welfare of all students in a school, not just their friends. Finally, student action or inaction depends on adults' ability to be effective bystanders themselves. No one is perfect, and adults won't always act against injustice, but it is important that they strive to be positive role models in this regard.

The remainder of this book will focus on specific techniques for building empathy, social problem solving skills, and positive peer culture in order to make positive and effective bystander action more likely. Long-lasting bullying prevention programs rely on students' gaining the knowledge, skills, motivation, and feelings of self-efficacy to partner with adults to make their schools safe and inclusive.

Chapter 2

The Foundations of Bullying Prevention Programs

The [Olweus bullying prevention] program strives to develop a school (and ideally a home) environment characterized by:

Warmth, positive interest, and involvement by adults

Firm limits to unacceptable behavior

Non-hostile, nonphysical negative consequences consistently applied in cases of . . . unacceptable behavior. . . .

Where adults act as authorities and positive role models.

—Olweus, Limber, and Milhalic (1997)

The strategies outlined in this book, or any student-based interventions to reduce bullying, have an important prerequisite: a consistent, schoolwide, staff-based bullying prevention program. Without positive role-modeling and mentoring by staff and consistent disciplinary actions focused on helping aggressive youth change, the techniques discussed in this book are unlikely to be effective. As I describe in detail in my first book, *Schools Where Everyone Belongs,* and as Rigby (n.d.) states:

Reports indicate that success is more likely to be achieved when [bullying prevention programs] are . . . applied thoroughly. . . . What constitutes thoroughness?

1. An anti-bullying policy and associated program is carefully formulated and is communicated to all members of the school community.

2. Members of the school community accept responsibility for carrying out the program—and do so. In particular:

- Work is done on bullying with children in classes as part of a planned curriculum.

- There is thoughtful attention continually paid to how children relate to each other, especially when there are indications that bullying is taking place.

- Action is consistently taken to deal with cases of bullying in accordance with an agreed policy.

Thorough implementation is likely to occur when:

Teachers care about the problem of bullying (Hence the need for surveys and subsequent discussion).

Teachers are meaningfully involved in the development of anti-bullying policy and know what they are expected to do.

Leadership in a school produces a "whole school approach" in which coordinated activities to address bullying actually occur (p. 2).

CHALLENGING MISPERCEPTIONS, DISCARDING INEFFECTIVE STRATEGIES

The first steps in bullying prevention are to challenge common misperceptions surrounding bullying and discard ineffective intervention strategies. Until the 1980s, bullying was often seen as a normal and acceptable part of childhood. Targets were advised to ignore the bullying, stand up for themselves, and understand that bullies were "just jealous." When adults began to realize that bullying was not inevitable and did in fact have negative effects on the young people involved, the first interventions emphasized telling aggressive youth about the negative impacts of bullying. Targets were instructed to tell bullies how they felt when bullied, use humor to deflect bullying, or "just walk away." Katherine Newman discusses the shortcomings of these strategies in her excellent book *Rampage: The Social Roots of School Shootings*. She writes:

Efforts to focus on changing either the bullies or the victims are unlikely to be effective. . . . The desire to behave better . . . is a weak motivator compared to the status gains that come from teasing and harassment. . . . Victims have no real way out of these situations because their low status makes most of the recommended strategies . . . ineffective. (2004, p. 293)

Teachers, parents, and students across the United States have reported to me that they have observed increases in bullying after schoolwide presentations that focused primarily on the negative effects of bullying. When these presentations are not accompanied by consistent behavioral expectations and consequences, youth who bully in order to gain power over others may become more aware of the power bullying can provide. One high school student wrote, in a 2006 survey I conducted, "We have had many assemblies to try and stop bullying, but most of the time it just gets worse. Most of the actual kids that are making fun of people just sit there and laugh."

Starting in the mid-1990s, many antibullying programs began to focus on schoolwide, staff-based interventions and changes in peer culture. These programs worked to build clear behavioral expectations, strengthen staff-student connections, and encourage bystanders to take action against bullying. The work of Olweus (1993, 2001), Ross (2003), Sharp and Smith (1994), and Pepler and Craig (2001) document the effectiveness of this approach.

As we work toward schoolwide interventions, it is important to remember that many school staff retain historical misperceptions about bullying. I have found the most common misperception to be that aggressive youth have low self-esteem and would stop bullying others if they knew how painful their behavior was for targets. Almost equally common is the belief that targets cause bullying by being nonassertive, overreactive, or socially withdrawn. I have found the most effective technique to remedy these misperceptions to be a discussion of the close parallels between attitudes toward bullying and historical perceptions surrounding the causes of and responses to domestic violence and sexual harassment. Common responses to these problems have been to make excuses for the abuser and to blame the victim. Women abused by their spouses in the 1950s were likely to hear "He didn't mean to hurt you" or "He had a hard day at work." Women reporting sexual harassment in the 1960s were likely to hear "He didn't mean anything by it" or "That's just how men talk." Similarly, students tell me that when they report bullying, some adults tell them, "He is just jealous" or "I know she didn't mean any harm." Historically, the advice given to battered women has communicated that they are at fault for their abuser's aggression. Friends and family advised battered wives to avoid disagreements with their abusers in public or take cooking classes. Regarding instances of workplace sexual harassment, targets were often told that it was their flirtatious behavior or provocative clothing that was to blame for their aggressors' behavior.

Similarly, parents often report to me that educators have told them, "Your child brings this on himself" or "They only bully her because it bothers her so much." This type of advice can leave targets feeling that they are at fault for the harassment or bullying. I often encourage school staff to ask themselves one question before giving advice to youth who are bullied: "Would I give the same advice to a target of workplace sexual harassment or domestic violence?" This question can help us recognize the messages implied by the advice we give young people.

Most people now recognize the unfairness and ineffectiveness of historical responses to domestic violence and sexual harassment, but similar attitudes prevail in cases of bullying. Both adults and students can benefit from a discussion of historical and cultural parallels to bullying in schools. From these discussions, adults often gain a deeper understanding of causes, effects, and effective and fair interventions. Students often gain an understanding of the importance of bullying prevention work, a sense of the applicability of what they are learning, and knowledge of specific and effective interventions.

COMMITMENT TO CHANGE

Clear commitment to change by administrators and staff is essential to effective bullying prevention programs. As Rigby's quotation at the beginning of this chapter suggests, thorough implementation and staff buy-in are essential elements. First, staff must recognize bullying as a problem in their school and care about creating change. Some potential initial activities that foster this attitude include a book discussion group, student and staff surveys and discussion of the results, and viewing and discussing a video such as *Let's Get Real*, directed by Debra Chasnoff (2004) and available from Women's Educational Media (www.womedia.org).

Beyond Staff Training

For bullying prevention programs to be successful, staff training is important but not sufficient. It is important for school staff to take ownership of the program; success is less likely when staff see the program as belonging to an outside trainer or organization. Staff and administrators must spend time examining and revising existing practices, developing new ways of preventing and reacting to bullying, and working toward consistency among all staff members. In effective programs, staff members see bullying prevention not as an add-on but as part of their school's basic responsibility to provide a safe learning environment for all students. Since in-the-moment staff reactions to student bullying do more to shape a school's culture than activities and presentations, success relies on active and engaged staff who pay attention to how students interact with one another and intervene when appropriate.

Administrators must actively support this effort and provide time, backup, and resources for the program. It is often helpful to commit to a specific implementation timeline so everyone involved is aware from the beginning of the time and resources required to follow through with the program. A timeline can also help schools track progress toward goals.

Creating a Bullying Prevention Team

Olweus (2001) found that creating a bullying prevention team of staff, administrators, and community members increases the probability of lasting change. This team can be the staff's on-site resource and guide for implementation by participating in monthly meetings to work out details, plan training and other events, monitor the progress of the intervention, and identify problems needing attention. The bullying prevention team can help staff maintain change over time by giving specific positive feedback and scheduling regular follow-up discussions.

Parent and Community Involvement

Parent and community involvement and support are also important and should be sought by involving parents in program planning, informing them about program development, and seeking their feedback as the program progresses. Interactions with the larger community should focus on incorporating parents' ideas and values, communicating data and plans, and monitoring interventions to ensure that the school follows through on promises for action. Schools can help parents support youth who bully, youth who are bullied, and bystanders.

A CONSISTENT DISCIPLINE SYSTEM

Essential to a successful bullying prevention program is a consistent discipline system for peer-to-peer aggressive behavior. Effective discipline begins with staff consensus about behavioral expectations. It is important for staff to work together to determine which aggressive behaviors will be deemed unacceptable and, of those behaviors, which ones staff will deal with in the moment and which ones staff will refer to administrators. Once there is staff-wide consensus about expectations, the next step is to implement a consistent, transparent discipline process and set of consequences. Students will be better able to change negative behaviors when they know in advance what the school's behavioral expectations are, what process is followed when students break rules, and what consequences will follow each category of unacceptable behavior. Consequences should start small and escalate slowly, and staff should maintain a positive feeling tone throughout the discipline process.

A Reflection Process

An effective bullying prevention program should include interventions to help aggressive youth create and internalize new ways of behaving. In *Schools Where Everyone Belongs,* I discuss one such intervention. This intervention uses the following four structured reflection questions:

- What did you do?
- What was wrong with that?
- What goal were you trying to reach?
- The next time you have that goal, how will you reach it without hurting someone else?

This process of reflection should be integrated into the school's discipline system. Some aggressive students will also need family or individual therapy, social skills training, or other interventions to help them meet their needs in more productive ways. It is crucial to build strong, positive, and collaborative relationships with parents of aggressive youth. As we empower the often overwhelmed parents of aggressive youth to take a more effective role in their children's lives, change becomes more likely.

Support for Targets

Messages for targets of bullying abound. The most common advice for targets includes standing up to youth who bully, walking away from a bullying incident, hiding the fact that the bullying bothers them, and the contradictory advice of telling bullies how the behavior makes them feel. In my experience working with countless targets of bullying, I have found the previous strategies often ineffective and sometimes even actively harmful. All these forms of advice risk communicating to targets that the bullying is caused by some failure or deficiency on their part.

In my view, we should advise targets of bullying to change their behavior only if they clearly did something wrong. This does not include telling an introvert to be an extrovert or telling an anxious child to stop being anxious. When students are anxious and overreactive as the result of continued bullying, we can help them calm themselves so they feel better. However, we should not imply to students that their anxiety-based overreactivity causes the bullying. When we focus our messages to targets on what they can do to minimize the bullying, we risk teaching them to blame themselves for another person's chosen behavior.

To replace the messages and advice outlined in the previous paragraph, we should strive to impart the messages summarized in the following quote:

> Bullying is WRONG. Nobody has the right to hurt other people by hitting them, kicking them, calling them names, spreading rumours about them or by doing anything else which is intended to be upsetting. Bullies try to justify their actions by saying that it is their victim's fault for being different. They may pick on someone who is tall or small, or fat or thin, or wears glasses, or has a different accent, or another religion, or is shy or clever, or good looking, or disabled. . . . Any excuse will do, and if there is no real difference then the bullies will invent one. If this is happening to you tell yourself that it is not your fault, and that it is the bullies who need to change, not you. (Scottish Executive, 1999, para. 1–3)

The core message we should emphasize to targets is that it is not their fault that they are bullied. Youth who bully choose their behavior, and any real or imagined differences targets possess do not make them deserve pain. We can advise targets of bullying to take the following actions instead:

- Ask for help and protection from adults and peers.
- Find ways to leave bullying situations, with someone else if possible.
- Ask bullies to stop, but don't be surprised if they don't listen.
- Record details in order to report them to adults.
- Use hobbies, calm breathing, and time with friends to heal themselves.

Two excellent resources for helping students heal are the work of Sanford (1992) and Dweck (2005). When we do see targets display behaviors that increase bullying, such as antisocial or aggressive behavior or when they stay in abusive friendships, we can help them gain skills to change these behaviors.

STAFF-STUDENT CONNECTIONS

Strong staff-student connections are essential to effective bullying prevention programs. In 2005, I surveyed 480 students at a Maine middle school. We asked students, among other things, how safe they felt in school and how many staff members they had positive relationships with. Seven percent of the students reported that they felt unsafe at school. Though 9 percent of all students surveyed reported that they had no positive relationships with staff, 45 percent of the students who said they felt unsafe at school also reported having no positive relationships with staff. This finding points strongly to the importance of building mentoring connections with all students.

Research on resiliency consistently finds that connection with positive adults is a key factor in recovery from any traumatic event. In addition, aggressive youth are more likely to change within the context of positive relationships with school staff. As Benard writes:

> The presence of at least one caring person—someone who conveys an attitude of compassion, who understands that no matter how awful a child's behavior, the child is doing the best he or she can given his or her experience—provides support for healthy development and learning. . . . An ethic of caring is obviously not a "program" or "strategy" per se, but rather a way of being in the world, a way of relating to youth, their families, and each other that conveys compassion, understanding, respect, and interest. (1995, para. 6)

In order to increase the likelihood of building connections with students, staff can identify and consciously reach out to students whom no staff member has a positive relationship with and make an effort to maintain positive feeling tone with all students. Building relationships with students is made more likely when staff and students have frequent opportunities to engage in mutually enjoyable activities. These may happen during homeroom times, class meetings, advisor-advisee times, or activity periods. All students—whether they behave as bullies, targets, or bystanders—are more likely to feel safe in school and learn new behaviors when they have positive relationships with school staff.

Using frequent praise of the kind supported by research helps adults form connections with students while also helping students repeat desired behaviors and discard undesired behaviors. Effective praise focuses young people's attention on their own actions and the natural positive consequences of those actions, instead of on their personality traits or adults' feelings (Deci & Flaste, 1996; Dweck, 2000, 2005; Kohn, 1999). This type of praise reinforces the possibility of change and encourages cause-and-effect thinking.

There is good reason to question the frequent use of I-messages, such as "I'm happy that you're doing your work" or "I'm disappointed that you hit Sheila." As Bluestein writes in her 2003 article, "What's Wrong With I-Messages?" when we tell young people we are happy or disappointed about their actions, we run the real risk of communicating to young people that they have control over and are responsible for our emotions. Bluestein points out another risk of using I-messages: "Additionally, these kinds of statements build dependence on external approval, teaching children to choose their behaviors on the basis of other people's potential reactions and opinions" (p. 2). Change initiated by a desire to please adults is unlikely to be long-lasting. More information about the effective use of praise can be found in *Schools Where Everyone Belongs*.

STAFF CODE OF CONDUCT

Day-to-day staff behavior has a profound impact on the emotional atmosphere of a school. Students notice how staff talk with one another, what they do or fail to do when other staff members are disrespectful, and inequalities in their treatment of students. This is an important issue, given that 93 percent of 236 current and former high school students surveyed reported seeing teachers exhibiting bullying behaviors toward students. McEvoy writes:

In many schools—perhaps most schools—at least one or more teachers can be identified as abusive towards students. . . . Simply stated, the faculty and students within the institution often are in private agreement about who the few culprits are, and express deep frustration at feeling powerless to stop the problematic behavior. (2005, p. 9)

Reducing teacher bullying begins with staff discussions about acceptable and unacceptable behaviors. These discussions may lead to consensus on a staff code of conduct. The code of conduct may address types of language, motivational techniques, approaches to discipline, and other teaching strategies. While maintaining flexibility for different teachers to use their own styles, school staff should work together with parents and students to determine which practices they consider unprofessional or destructive. Even when a discussion of unacceptable practices does not lead to a formal code of conduct, it can still be beneficial because it builds awareness of what behaviors colleagues find unacceptable.

The next step is to determine what actions to take when one staff member observes another staff member displaying unacceptable behaviors. Staff in one school that I worked with created a code phrase for staff to use to alert one another when they were talking inappropriately with students. Staff members can give one another permission to inform them immediately or after the fact if they are acting in an unacceptable manner. Administrators should make it clear that they expect staff to report inappropriate behavior and will take seriously and investigate thoroughly complaints from staff or students about aggressive or unacceptable behavior displayed by any staff member.

CULTURAL AWARENESS

Diversity training for staff members can help them become aware of practices that convey unintended meanings to young people from diverse backgrounds. Many gestures, words, and actions have different meanings in different cultures. The more we understand the expectations and communication styles of our students and their families, the more able we are to avoid the frustration that can arise from cultural misunderstanding. It is helpful to note that even schools initially seen as homogenous are diverse in meaningful ways. In rural Maine, where I work, there is currently little ethnic and racial diversity. Equally significant are differences in gender, socioeconomic status, and sexual orientation. By exploring questions of diversity in every setting, we can begin to understand the different thought processes and needs of the communities we serve. It is important for staff to strive to recognize their own strengths, weaknesses, and biases in this regard. Even in schools where there is little racial diversity, we can and should address staff attitudes and behaviors toward boys and girls, youth from different income levels, and youth and adults of different sexual orientations. When subconscious attitudes become conscious, we become better able to recognize and change biased behaviors. Fair, kind, and consistent behavior among staff is essential for students to feel safe and empowered to create a positive peer culture.

Because I have worked in rural Maine schools with little racial diversity for many years, I have not included many specific activities to address race and ethnicity in this book. I believe that the techniques described here can be used in discussing these important issues as well. Recommended resources for focusing on race and culture include

> *Beyond Heroes and Holidays: A Practical Guide to K–12 Multicultural, Anti-Racist Education and Staff Development* (2nd ed.), edited by E. Lee, D. Menkart, and M. Okazawa-Rey (Washington, DC: Teaching for Change, 2002).

> *From Rage to Hope: Strategies for Reclaiming Black and Hispanic Students* (2nd ed.), by C. Kuykendall (Bloomington, IN: National Educational Service, 2004).

> *The Middle of Everywhere,* by M. Pipher (New York: Harcourt, 2002).

> *Making the Peace: A 15-Session Violence Prevention Curriculum for Young People,* by P. Kivel and A. Creighton (Alameda, CA: Hunter House, 1997).

SUMMARY AND CONCLUSIONS

The first step in developing effective bullying prevention programs is to make schools safe places for all students. To meet this end, school staff should develop clear, enforced, school-wide standards of acceptable and unacceptable behavior with predictable and consistent consequences. In addition, positive modeling by staff and strong staff-student relationships encourage appropriate behavior and make it more likely that young people will report bullying. Schools should help aggressive youth change their behavior and find other ways to meet their needs. Support for targets of bullying should focus on protection, connection, and healing, rather than on advice. It is only after these interventions are in place that we can empower student bystanders to tackle the problem of bullying, develop empathy and skills, and consciously implement positive school culture.

Chapter 3

Building Empathy and Social Problem Solving Skills

As early as preschool, children can learn to identify an interpersonal problem . . . to think of their own and others' feelings, to consider alternative solutions to solving an interpersonal problem . . . and to understand potential consequences of acts.

—*Shure (2006)*

Much of my work with young people focuses on building and mastering skills. This focus comes in large part from the work of Steve Danish (Danish & Gullotta, 2000). He writes that we have three options when implementing prevention programs. First, we could focus on providing information by telling young people how important bullying prevention is, how deeply bullying affects others, and what they should do when they observe or experience bullying. As Danish points out, this style of intervention is easy to implement but unlikely to change student behavior. Second, we could focus on changing values and attitudes. Danish writes that while changed values may lead to changed behavior, making such changes is a difficult, long-term process. Third, we could focus on teaching skills. Mastery of skills is more likely to lead to behavior change than providing information and is easier to achieve than a fundamental change in values.

Teaching skills also requires different techniques than teaching knowledge or changing values. Danish writes:

> Skills are taught differently than knowledge, attitudes, or values. Just as learning to drive a car, dance, or play a sport cannot occur solely through listening to a tape or reading a

39

book, skills for living cannot be taught in a passive manner. A Chinese proverb states: I listen—and forget. I see—and remember. I do—and understand. (2000, p. 283)

Similarly, Bligh writes:

If students are to learn to think, they must be placed in situations where they have to do so. The situations in which they are obliged to think are those in which they have to answer questions, because questions demand an active mental response. . . . The best way to learn to solve problems is to be given problems that have to be solved. (2000, p. 10)

In this chapter, I will discuss classroom and in-the-moment techniques to increase empathy and social problem solving skills in young people. Many of these techniques can be applied to topics addressed in the remainder of the book.

CLASSROOM MANAGEMENT

Before detailing techniques for teaching social problem solving skills, it is worthwhile to outline some essential classroom management guidelines to ensure students' safety. Without a safe and accepting classroom environment, students are unlikely to develop empathy and learn skills they will use in the future.

Preventing and Dealing with Disruption by Aggressive Students

First, we should set bystanders as our target audience. As I will discuss in chapter 5, the majority of young people are kind and sympathetic. Students who repeatedly act aggressively toward peers are in the minority. While it may seem that aggressive students need our lessons the most, classroom discussions are usually not enough to inspire real change in them. Youth who act aggressively toward others may attempt to seize power during classroom discussions about bullying by distracting or insulting others. If aggressive students repeatedly disrupt classroom discussions or make them unsafe for others in the classroom, we should remove those students from the classroom temporarily so the rest of the class can benefit from the lessons.

When we incorporate constant review into our lessons, students can be asked to leave, return for the next lesson, and still receive the same instruction.

Establishing Rules

We should make rules clear from the start. We should not allow students to use classroom lessons to discuss actual conflicts between named children or actual incidents of bullying. They can talk about real events as long as the events and the identities of the students involved are sufficiently disguised to protect the feelings of those who were bullied and to avoid the real risk that a discussion of bullying will become a reenactment of past aggression. When discussing emotions, we should set boundaries and choose questions carefully to discourage students from bringing up private family business in the public classroom forum.

Interrupting, hitting, or criticizing others' ideas should also be forbidden. When students break these rules, we may or may not give them a second chance, depending on their behavior. We can place a chair away from the group but still in the room and send those who break rules to sit in this chair. If students continue to interrupt or act aggressively, we can send them to a partner classroom or to the office. Before separating students from the class, we can approach them with a choice. With a positive feeling tone, we quietly ask, for example, "Albert, you have a choice. You can stop interrupting and stay here, or you can sit in the back of the room. Which do you want to do?" Most of the time, students will choose to stop interrupting. If they continue to interrupt, we should not hesitate to send them to the back of the room or to a prearranged location in the school.

Modeling Inclusion and Having Fun

We should model inclusion in the ways we call on students and pick volunteers. It is important to involve all students in discussions, even those who are naturally more reserved. We can use a variety of fair and random methods to choose volunteers and assign groups, including choosing by birthday, having students draw sticks from a jar, and lining students up to count off by number. When students complain, we can explain that they are only allowed to complain if something isn't fair—not if they don't get what they want. When students point out bona fide unfairness, we should thank them and alter our methods. Besides clear expectations and a model of fairness, fun is also an essential element. Fun and frequent specific praise make students want to stay in the room and be involved while also encouraging them to look forward to the next session.

Building Empathy

Once we have set ground rules and have procedures in place for enforcing them, we can begin focusing on the content of our discussions. The first step to foster effective social problem solving skills in young people is to build empathy. Feshbach (1983) gives a three-part definition of empathy: "the capacity to discriminate and identify an emotional state in another, the ability to assume the perspective and role of another person, and the ability to respond affectively [that is, to respond to others' emotions with parallel emotions of our own]" (p. 267). As Upright (2002) notes: "Empathy, the ability to care about others, is a learned process" (p. 15). Helping young people develop empathy has wide-ranging positive consequences for individuals and schools. When students understand and care about others' feelings, they are more likely to treat peers in kind ways. Empathetic students reach out to others and act spontaneously to make their classrooms, schools, families, and communities more inclusive.

Empathy, like social problem solving, consists of skills to be developed rather than a set of appropriate responses to be learned. Feshbach describes an empathy training program geared toward the management of aggressive behavior in the classroom:

> The training content does not focus on discouraging aggressive behaviors, nor does it attempt to reward manifestations of empathy. What are valued, trained and reinforced are the child's ability to perceive situations from the perspective of other people, to discriminate and identify feelings, and to express feelings that he or she may be experiencing. It is

assumed that through the training of these skills, the child's range of alternative behaviors becomes expanded, and possibilities other than aggressive and egocentric reactions become available in the child's behavioral repertoire. . . . The children are rewarded for the variety of solutions they verbalize, not for offering any particular solution, even if it be the socially desirable one. (1983, p. 269)

We begin building empathy by teaching students to be aware of and understand their own emotions. I agree with Cotton (2001) when she writes:

When seeking to increase the ability of children to assume another's perspective, it is most fruitful to have them focus first on their own feelings—the different kinds of feelings they have and what feelings are associated with what kinds of situations.

We can start this learning process in kindergarten, or even earlier, by teaching students to identify a wide range of emotions. Many students I meet arrive at school with a two-word feelings vocabulary. When asked how they feel, they respond, "bad" or "good." In order for young people to act appropriately and effectively when they experience different emotions, it is essential that they learn to differentiate between the many emotions that can be lumped into these two categories. For example, students who say they feel bad may actually be feeling worried, scared, angry, or sad. Students who feel good may actually be feeling happy, excited, proud, or grateful. Being able to distinguish one feeling from another allows students to gain understanding and choose actions to express and resolve their feelings.

One of the ways we can push students to see beyond good and bad is by drawing parallels to the ways in which we describe weather and food. We can ask them what we would learn if someone told us the weather during recess was good. Students typically reply that we would learn that the sun was out and the air was warm. We can point out that individuals who like the rain might describe the weather as good when it was raining. Thus saying, "It's raining" or "It's sunny," provides more information. We can draw a parallel to descriptions of food by asking if portraying food as good or bad can tell us if it is spicy, crunchy, sweet, or soft. Once we have this discussion a few times, we can respond to the answer "good" with "Good happy, good proud, good excited, or good grateful?" Over time, students learn to use more precise descriptions for their feelings, and will be able to react to those specific feelings in more effective ways.

We can transition from helping young people identify their own emotions to helping them understand others' emotions by deepening and expanding our discussions. I often present students with photographs of children's faces and ask them to identify those children's feelings. I act out emotions with my face and body and have students act out emotions for one another. We can ask where in their bodies children experience sadness, anger, pride, or fear; what they have done when they experience these feelings; and how they can identify these same feelings in others. As young people hear that others in their class feel sad in situations in which they would feel angry, they can begin to understand that others may have different feelings than they do in the same situations. As Upright explains, in the context of discussing moral dilemmas from books, "This disagreement is essential. Over time, it will increase empathy as students learn to objectively listen to, understand, and respect the ideas of others" (2002, p. 19).

Emotions and Actions

Another discussion topic for helping students understand both their own and others' emotions is the range of possible actions related to each emotion. Through brainstorming, improvisational theater, and discussion, we can help students develop effective techniques for dealing with sadness, anger, fear, and worry. For example, we can help young people differentiate between realistic and unrealistic fears and take realistic fears seriously while calming themselves when they experience unrealistic fears. Similarly, we can help students distinguish between sadness from a real loss and sadness from not getting what they want. Young people can learn to cope with sadness from the death of a pet or loss of a friend by thinking about something else, remembering good times, talking with someone, going for a walk, or writing a letter to the pet or person. Young people can learn to cope with sadness from not getting what they want by taking a breath and moving on. When dealing with anger, I have found it ineffective to teach young people to "let their anger out" by hitting a pillow, for instance. Instead, I strive to teach students to solve problems connected to their anger, use self-calming techniques, and ask adults for help.

Specific techniques for dealing with different emotions will vary from individual to individual. When students see that how they deal with their emotions is different from the way their classmates do, they begin to understand their classmates in a deeper way. Learning that there are many different positive actions to take when feeling angry, sad, lonely, excited, or embarrassed introduces students to a view of life in which they can experiment with solutions until they find one that works.

Using Literature

Literature is uniquely useful to build empathy because we can discuss someone's feelings in detail without invading the privacy of a real person. By teaching through literature, we strike a balance between the abstract and distant cognitive strategies of worksheets and the immediate and emotional strategies of talking about real people and personal issues. When we talk about the feelings of fictional characters young people have grown to care for, our strategies become immediate and emotional, but not too personal. Our efforts will be more productive when we spend the time to embark on in-depth discussions, structure opportunities for students to act out scenes in a book and brainstorm possible solutions to problems the characters encounter, and focus on how the book applies to students' own lives.

When using literature as a tool to build empathy, we can begin by asking questions about the plot and setting to make sure students understand what is happening in the book. We can ask students to compare the cultural setting of the book to their own lives. As we read aloud from the book, we should stop periodically to ask questions and thus deepen students' understanding of and connection to the book and the characters. We can ask students how characters in the story are feeling and push them to describe those feelings concretely and specifically. We can also ask students to use the words in the text, the illustrations, and their own experiences to predict what the characters will do next. We can thoroughly discuss words, phrases, and the subtle connotations of language, events, and ideas in the book. We should often put the book aside to have students act out scenes and thus further deepen their understanding of and empathy for characters.

Learning about others' feelings through moving and acting like them and thus discovering from the inside how they feel is a technique based on the work of the internationally known mime and acting teacher Tony Montanaro (1995). We can present acting in this context as an opportunity to discover what it's like to be someone else. We should continually strive to connect our book discussions to students' own lives by asking, "How does the book parallel real situations at our school?" and "What have you done in similar situations?" or "What could you do in similar situations?" We discuss the real choices students make in their own lives and strive to understand how those choices affect others and what other options for behavior exist. Finally, in order to cement learning, we can encourage students to make our work their own by teaching others what they have learned from our discussions.

Following is a short list of some of the books I have found useful in my work with young people:

A Day's Work, by E. Bunting (Clarion, 1991).

Fly Away Home, by E. Bunting and R. Himler (Clarion, 1994).

Because of Winn-Dixie, by K. DiCamillo (Candlewick Press, 2000).

The Hundred Dresses, by E. Estes (Harcourt, 2004/1944).

Follow My Leader, by J. Garfield (Viking Press, 1957).

Rosa, by N. Giovanni (Henry Holt, 2005).

My Secret Bully, by T. Ludwig (Riverwood Press, 2003).

Just Kidding, by T. Ludwig (Tricycle Press, 2006).

Bridge to Terabithia, by K. Paterson (HarperTrophy, 1978).

The Great Gilly Hopkins, by K. Paterson (HarperTrophy, 1979).

Character Counts: Children's Books That Build Character (Josephson Institute, n.d.) and *Gender Issues in Children's Literature* (Singh, 1998) are helpful resources for choosing books. Additionally, McGowan, McGowan, and Wheeler's 1994 book, *Appreciating Diversity through Children's Literature: Teaching Activities for the Primary Grades*, is a useful resource for choosing and using literature to help young people celebrate diversity. A word of caution: When choosing books about bullying, we should be wary of stories in which targets of bullying use counteraggression to solve their problems, especially when targets are portrayed as enjoying the pain they inflict on the bully.

A detailed set of lessons for using Eleanor Estes's book *The Hundred Dresses* to build empathy and encourage effective bystander action appears as Appendix B. The following example from my work using *The Hundred Dresses* shows one way to expand a discussion of literature when students struggle to understand the motivations and feelings of certain characters. My hope is that you find the techniques presented here and in Appendix B applicable to a variety of literature-based classroom discussions.

In *The Hundred Dresses*, one of the main characters, Wanda, comes from a low-income home. She lies to a popular child, telling her that she has 100 dresses at home. The popular student responds by teasing her, and their peers laugh. My students are often puzzled by Wanda's choice to lie about how many dresses she has. In order to help them understand Wanda's actions, I propose the following parallel example:

> Imagine that I am a student whose family just barely has enough money for rent and food. We save for months for special treats, such as going out to a movie. We can't afford to buy popcorn at the movies, so we bring in bags of snacks under our coats. Imagine that your families take you to Disneyworld every year. For a month before and after the trip, Disneyworld is all you talk about. I hear all about the rides, food, plane trip, and the hotel you will stay in.

I then play the role of the low-income student and ask for volunteers to play the roles of other students, excitedly talking about Disneyworld. In my role, I listen to their conversation with a look of longing and desire. I slowly approach the students talking about Disneyworld and say, shyly, "I like the Space Mountain ride the best. I went down it six times." At this point, I end the scene to ask the class, "What just happened?"

"You lied," they reply. I acknowledge this and agree with them that lying is wrong, but then I ask if this kind of lie is different from lying to their parents about breaking a lamp or to their peers by spreading a mean rumor. They tell me that this lie is different because of my intention. Instead of lying to shirk responsibility or gain control over others, I lied because I wanted to belong. We return to the acting scenario to experiment with ways in which young people can productively respond to these situations. Often, the first solution they test is to say flat out to my character, "That's a lie." I ask the class to consider the impact of this statement, and they realize that it would make my character feel even worse. Only after realizing that it is not their job to make me tell the truth do they begin to experiment with more effective solutions. They practice saying, "Yeah, I like that one, too," and changing the subject or including me in a game so I won't feel left out. They also discuss talking less about material belongings and vacations in the first place. By creating an example more immediately relevant to my students' lives, we can help them better understand the actions of the character Wanda, as well as how they can react to similar actions in their own lives. Parallel opportunities to make the dilemmas presented in books or in historical situations real to students often present themselves.

Persona Dolls

Another promising practice in developing empathy in young children involves the use of persona dolls ("Welcome to Persona Doll Training," n.d.), an approach originating in the United Kingdom. Each doll has a unique story, complete with family background and likes and dislikes. Adults bring these dolls to visit classrooms, and young people get to know the dolls, discovering how they are similar to and different from each doll.

These similarities and differences include ethnic background, likes and dislikes, family composition, and abilities and disabilities. As students learn that others who appear quite different from them also share important traits and experiences, they begin to develop a true appreciation for diversity.

Public Service

We can also teach empathy by providing opportunities for generosity and public service, especially when service is designed to help students learn about the needs and lives of others. Service projects can help young people learn about others when we discuss why we are helping, invite students to understand the challenges others face, and encourage students to see the profound impact their actions can have on alleviating others' struggles. Possible community service projects include saving pennies for charities, cleaning up the playground, tutoring or otherwise helping peers or younger students, planning a food drive, working in a soup kitchen, and helping build houses. In the community where I work, our students contribute more than half of the food distributed by the local food bank. Students at the Bean school proudly make graphs showing how their efforts help relieve hunger in their community. Each year, the student council makes a video during which it discusses why we collect food. In 2006, the student council created a slogan for our annual food drive: "We share because we care." As a school community, we talk openly about why we do not award prizes to the students who bring in the most food, instead preferring for each student to bring in at least one food item and to find motivation from knowing that he or she is helping others. As Brendtro, Brokenleg, and Van Bockern write in *Reclaiming Youth at Risk,* "Without opportunities to give to others, young people do not develop as caring persons" (1990, p. 50).

Maintaining an Affective Element

Throughout our work building empathy, we should be careful to maintain a strong affective element to our discussions. When we treat empathy building as a cognitive activity—based solely on pictures and language and without discussion about the experience of feeling sad or scared—we risk making it easier for young people who bully to learn to manipulate their targets. When we focus on both affective and cognitive empathy, it is more likely that students will learn not only to be aware of others' feelings, but also to care about them.

In the context of using literature to teach students to value diversity, McGowan et al. (1994) recommend three sets of activities: activities of the head, based on learning and processing information; activities of the hand, focused on building and using skills; and activities of the heart, focused on building beliefs. Adult role-modeling is essential to meeting this goal. Adults who show caring toward students help them care for their peers. Greeting and goodbye rituals, during which teachers focus on each individual student with warmth and enthusiasm, are especially helpful in our interactions with students whom we have difficulty liking. Adults should establish and reinforce positive social norms by frequently noticing, encouraging, and praising acts of concern, helping, and inclusion. As Feshbach writes, "There is an interesting and important relationship between empathy and attachment" (1983, p. 269). We promote the mutually reinforcing skills of empathy and attachment when we strive to form positive relationships with all students and structure our lessons to encourage students to form attachments with a wide range of their peers.

SOCIAL PROBLEM SOLVING SKILLS

The methods described here are based in large part on the work of Shure (Shure & Spivack, 1982, Shure, 2001a–c), O'Neill (O'Neill & Glass, 2000), and McCarthy (1987). Shure's work taught me to focus on empowering students to create their own solutions to social problems. She describes her method, Interpersonal Cognitive Problem Solving (ICPS), as follows:

> We have many ways of changing the poor behavior of young children. We can tell them what to do and what not to do. We can explain why our idea is a good one. We can model, coach or ignore and hope that what they do will go away. But these approaches are essentially the same—we are doing the

thinking for children. . . . ICPS is different. We introduce problem solving techniques to children. We do not teach children what to think or do, but how to think so they can resolve problems successfully with peers and authority figures. (Shure, 1995, p. 4)

Shure emphasizes that when we involve young people in finding their own solutions to problems, they are more likely to use those solutions, and they learn an approach to problem solving that they can apply during the rest of their lives. When students learn to generate many possible solutions for any given problem, they develop a mental flexibility that allows them to choose a different solution when the first doesn't work.

Shure advocates for teaching young people three specific steps for social problem solving. First, students identify the problem and generate many possible solutions. They then predict the outcome of each solution and choose one based on the predicted outcomes. Finally, students monitor outcomes to gauge the effectiveness of the chosen solution. When students report the outcome as positive, they are encouraged to use the solution again; when students report the outcome as negative, they are encouraged to try a different solution from their list.

Differentiating Big Problems from Small Problems

The curriculum outlined in *Kelso's Choice: Conflict Management Skills* (O'Neill & Glass, 2000) helps students differentiate between big problems, which they should ask adults for help on right away, and small problems, which they should try to solve several times themselves before approaching adults for help. This distinction helps emphasize problem-solving skills while also urging students to come to adults right away when they are targets or observers of bullying. Making the distinction between big and small problems is not easy for young people. It is not enough simply to tell them, "I only want you to come to me if it's a big deal." In addition, as students get older they become more proficient problem solvers, and some scenarios move from their big list to their small list. We can help students differentiate between big and small problems when we structure opportunities to act and discuss practice scenarios, point out their successes in problem solving, prompt them in the moment, and thank them for coming to adults for help, even if we then encourage them to try their own solutions. It is essential that adults listen to and help students who have tried two solutions for a small problem and found them unsuccessful.

Learning Styles

McCarthy's (1987) work on learning styles helps us use a wide range of teaching strategies to maximize comprehension and help students apply what they learn in real-life situations. McCarthy's work is a synthesis of the work of many researchers in the field of learning theory. She categorizes students according to four learning styles and recommends that educators structure their lessons to reach all four groups. She sequences instructional presentations so that students begin by discussing why the material they will learn is important to them. (We may also use storytelling or experiential exercises in this phase.) This, she writes, will reach learners who learn best when they understand the personal significance of the information and skills to be learned. Second, she suggests presenting fact- and research-based knowledge to address the needs of learners who learn best from authorities. Third, she recommends providing hands-on, experiential learners with a chance to practice. Finally, she advocates providing opportunities for students to modify and teach what they have learned in order to meet the needs of students who learn best when they have the chance to make the material their own.

Over the years, as I continue to follow McCarthy's recommendations, I have become convinced that *all* students benefit from instruction that targets all four learning styles. Instead of using McCarthy's sequence solely to reach students with varying learning styles, we can use the system to improve retention of learning for all students, increase the chances that students will use the skills and knowledge we teach them, and build deeper understanding. Traditional classroom teaching, which emphasizes McCarthy's second phase, carries the risk of teaching facts that do not broaden understanding or lead to lasting change.

A Combined Focus

We can use this combined focus on problem solving and learning styles in our work with adults and young people. The following pages describe specific techniques based on the work of Danish, Shure, O'Neill, and McCarthy to empower students to solve social problems effectively. While describing each technique, I will give specific examples. Please adapt the described lessons as you see fit. The sequence of techniques discussed is as follows:

- Taking advantage of teachable moments
- Helping students find personal significance
- Empowering students to create and take ownership for solutions
- Structuring adequate practice for students to reach mastery
- Providing opportunities for students to teach others
- Following up to assess implementation and refine lists of solutions

I will also discuss how these techniques apply specifically to discussions geared toward encouraging bystander action, including discussions about differentiated solutions for relational aggression.

Taking Advantage of Teachable Moments

Adult flexibility is essential to teaching social problem solving because the issues students present us with in the moment are often more important than the issues we plan to discuss. We may enter a lesson with a certain goal in mind and discard that goal because students' needs lead us in another direction. The following examples will show how to take advantage of teachable moments while encouraging the development of social problem solving skills.

One day at the Bean school, before I began a second-grade lesson on social problem solving skills, a classroom teacher led a recitation of the Pledge of Allegiance. Instead of moving directly into the planned discussion, I asked the class what the phrase "justice for all" meant to them. Not a single student had an accurate definition for the word *justice*. One student thought it had something to do with the army, while others said justice meant "American" or "nice." I told the students that justice was like another word they knew: *fairness*. We discussed what fairness means in schools and the ways in which they can treat one another fairly. In fourth or fifth grade, this discussion could have included a focus on popularity, differential treatment of individuals, and exclusion of marginalized subgroups. With upper grades, this discussion could also have provided an opportunity for students to give staff feedback about their fair and unfair behavior toward students. The second-grade discussion led to a new slogan for the school: "The James H. Bean School: With kindness and fairness for all."

A first grader wore his favorite pink and gray shirt to school one day in October. A circle of other first-grade boys laughed at him on the playground, saying, "Only girls wear pink." On my way home from school that day, I stopped to buy several pink shirts for myself. I talked with the first-grade boy the next day, and we planned to wear our pink shirts on the following day. On the following day, I visited the first-grade classrooms to say hello. Students pointed out the color of my shirt. I asked them if wearing a pink shirt made me a girl. They said no. I asked what happens when children laugh at each other, and we discussed how teasing makes targets feel bad. I encouraged them to look around the room and be glad that everyone wears different clothes because life would be boring if we all looked the same. I used this as a lead-in to a more in-depth discussion of individual differences and the value of diversity. During recess, several older students approached me, obviously puzzled. "Mr. Davis," they said, "girls wear pink." "That's right," I said, "so do boys." As I continued to wear my pink shirts for the following week, this brief and simple intervention led to numerous impromptu discussions in the halls about gender stereotypes. It became clear to me that when we pay attention, we can find many opportunities throughout any school year to remind young people that we are all different and that there are many ways to be male or female. When we hear boys criticized for showing feelings or girls called tomboys for being strong and athletic, we can challenge these statements in the moment and extend impromptu lessons through further discussion.

The water fountain at the Bean school was broken for several days, and students had to fill plastic cups at water coolers instead. This process took considerably longer than drinking from the water fountain and a class of kindergarten students grew impatient. A parent volunteer started to get cross with the students and said, "You have to wait quietly," in an angry tone of voice. This approach did not work, and the students became louder. An experienced teacher approached the scene and started singing quietly, "It's hard to wait, but we can do it. It's hard to wait. It's hard to wait." As she repeated this improvised song, the students started singing and calming down. While this may seem like an insignificant technique, used purely for crowd control, it actually teaches students an important lesson. The teacher emphasized strength instead of misbehavior and acknowledged how hard life can be for four- and five-year-olds.

I walked into a classroom, having planned a lesson about rumors, and I noticed two students wearing T-shirts with interesting messages. One shirt read, "I'm putting myself in charge," and the other, "Ask me if I care." Both students were empathetic, hard-working members of our school community, yet their shirts bore messages that could be seen as quite negative. Abandoning the lesson I had planned, I asked the whole class how the messages written on these two shirts could be seen as either positive or negative. They replied that "I'm putting myself in charge" could mean that I'm in charge of you, and you have to listen and obey. It could also mean that "I'm putting myself in charge" of myself, which would mean that I do my homework without being nagged, get myself up in the morning, and clean up after myself without being told. As we continued this discussion, I asked students how they take responsibility for themselves and how it makes them feel. The following week, I asked them for more examples of positive self-control at home and at school. When I asked about the second T-shirt, students replied that "Ask me if I care" could have two possible answers:

"No, I don't care" or "Yes, I do care." This naturally led to an extended discussion focused on what the students cared about. After they talked about their toys and families, I steered the conversation toward what they value in a school and how they can shape peer culture to achieve those values. As part of this discussion, we focused on my intended topic of rumors.

The preceding four examples show some of the benefits of adopting a flexible, question-based approach to teaching skills and encouraging positive peer culture. This approach requires one to observe, ask the right questions at the right times, and have the patience to extend lessons beyond the first questions and answers. Because these lessons will flow from the moment, not all will be successful. We will sometimes miss opportunities or ask the wrong questions. Yet when this approach works, it has the potential to lead to memorable learning experiences.

Helping Students Find Personal Significance

Fundamental to our lessons in social problem solving are questions such as "Why is this important?" and "When and how will we use these skills?" When asking these questions, we establish reasons for learning to solve the problems in question and make plans to put the solutions into practice. When addressing problem-solving techniques, we can ask, "Why is it important to have more than one solution for any problem?" When addressing bullying, we can ask, "What is bullying?" and "Why is it important to stop it?" Students' answers to these and other questions can open avenues for further discussion. Telling stories and discussing student reactions to brief video segments can help young people focus on why the skills they develop are important. We can also draw appropriate parallels to adult life, showing students how the skills they learn can aid them throughout their lives.

Discussing historical parallels to bullying can help students understand the far-reaching importance of building effective skills as bystanders. As I touched on in chapter 2, both adults and students can learn a great deal from looking at the parallels between bullying and other forms of social oppression. Discussing these parallels helps students become aware of the social and cultural forces that underlie bullying behavior and see how working to reduce bullying can help remedy the larger culture's acceptance of injustice toward marginalized populations. When we teach lessons about historical times of oppression and social activism, we can draw parallels to the bullying and exclusion of subgroups in our own schools. When we talk about individuals and groups who have made a difference, we can help students see what they can do to make a difference.

Depending on the needs, experience, and knowledge of staff and students, there are many topics we can discuss, including domestic violence, ethnic genocide, homophobia, racism, anti-immigrant sentiments, and discrimination against people with disabilities. One goal of these discussions should be to help students notice and understand the social environment of their own schools and see what they can do to limit exclusion and mistreatment of marginalized subgroups and individuals. Seeing the connections between historical attitudes and events and students' own attitudes and behaviors can help young people understand the importance of our lessons.

Empowering Students to Create and Take Ownership of Solutions

Many curricula exist for teaching positive social behavior. These curricula often include lists of problem-solving methods, rules for positive behavior, worksheets, stories, and practice activities. While they include a wide range of helpful activities, many curricula have one major weakness: They *tell* young people how to solve problems, get along, and build friendships. When students obediently memorize lists of rules and strategies, they seldom internalize or implement them. Without ownership and internalization, it is unlikely that students will use the strategies discussed in real-life situations. An additional difficulty presented by uniform, preset rules is that not all communities, schools, and students are the same. What may work in one context or for one individual may not work in another context or for another individual. When students and teachers cocreate and practice their own solutions to social problems, implementation in real-life situations becomes much more likely. We can draw on young people's life experiences by asking them about past problems, what solutions they tried, how those solutions worked, and how they could solve similar problems in the future. When we ask these questions, we help students recognize their past successes and gain confidence while also reflecting on and learning from past failures.

The following lesson is an example of one that derives content from students instead of a curriculum, therefore maximizing student ownership. For three years at the Bean school, we implemented the program outlined in *Kelso's Choice: Conflict Management Skills* (O'Neill & Glass, 2000). Besides helping young people differentiate between big and small problems, the Kelso's Choice curriculum outlines nine preset problem-solving solutions for students to use to resolve small problems. In 2006, I encouraged second graders at the Bean school to create their own content within the structure of the program. I used discussion to teach the key concepts, emphasizing that there are big and small problems, that they should tell adults about big problems and try to solve small problems themselves, and that almost all problems have many solutions. I then led four 30-minute lessons, during which we brainstormed a list of problems that second graders face and developed and tested possible solutions. These problems included having no one to play with, having someone call you names, having a friend break up with you, and many more. We practiced differentiating between big and small problems. For each small problem, we used improvisational theater and classroom discussion to test and fine-tune a wide range of brainstormed solutions. I returned to the second-grade classrooms on the fifth week with an incomplete list of successful solutions and asked students to remind me of the ones I had left out. Here is our final list of recommended solutions:

> We know that if we are kind and fair, most other people will be nice to us. When we have a big problem, we will tell an adult right away. When we have a small problem, we will try two of the following solutions before we tell an adult.
>
> 1. We can forget about it and move on. We can say, "Okay," or ignore what the other person did.

2. We can walk away—alone or with someone else.

3. When we have a problem with a friend, we can play with someone else for a while.

4. We can tell people in a nice way to stop.

5. When we are arguing about what to do together, we can make a deal.

6. We can calm ourselves when we are angry. We can do this by thinking before we talk, getting away for a minute, or taking a deep breath.

7. When we want to join a game, we can compliment the players first and then ask if we can play.

I will return to this series of lessons with the Bean school second graders throughout this chapter to show how using many teaching techniques can solidify and deepen understanding and make long-lasting change more likely.

One of the most effective strategies for empowering students to create their own solutions and take ownership of their learning is to use open-ended questions. I have found that successful open-ended questions help to encourage reflection, lack an obvious right answer, and help students focus on specifics. "Do you see that teasing hurts people?" is a closed question, which can be answered with a yes or no and obviously has a "right answer." This question and others like it do little to help students see and act differently. Many of the questions adults ask young people in school have right and wrong answers. While it is important for young people to learn specific academic skills and facts, we should remember that problems students face in the social realm are complex and have many solutions. Since open-ended questions have no single right answer, we should make sure we truly seek answers that are based on students' thinking each time we ask any particular question. It is important to welcome and affirm unexpected answers. If we become accustomed to the common answers, or the ones we personally agree with, we risk stealing ownership and empowerment from students. It can be easy to inadvertently communicate, verbally or nonverbally, that there are, in fact, right and wrong answers to our questions. When we do this, many of our students will strive to figure out our right answers instead of coming up with their own right answers.

Following is a short list of possible open-ended questions that can be useful when discussing social problem solving skills, what to do when observing bullying, and how to build a positive and inclusive peer culture. Before listing these questions, it is important to note that anytime we ask students to describe personal experiences or observations, we should prohibit the use of names or other identifying information. Over time, you will create other questions effective in your school and community. I encourage you to share with me the questions you develop:

- Tell me about a problem you saw at school. What did each person do? What happened next? How did it all turn out?

- What words have you heard people say that could hurt others?

- How do you think people feel when they hear these words?

- Tell me about a time when you saw someone stand up for someone else. What did he or she do? What happened next?

- Tell me about a time when someone told a teacher that someone was hurting someone else. What happened next?

- Tell me about a time when you wanted to stand up for someone but didn't. What stopped you? What could you do next time?

- Tell me about a time when someone helped you. What did the person do? What happened next?

- Tell me about a time when you helped someone else. What was the problem? What did you do? How do you think the person you helped felt? How did you feel?

- Tell me about a time when you almost hurt someone with words or actions. What did you almost do? What did you do instead? How did you make that decision?

- What does that word mean (because, fun, teasing, etc.)? Does the meaning change when you use it in this sentence? . . .

- What do your peers do to make school a safe place?
- What kind of school is this? What kind of school do you want it to be?
- What does this discussion have to do with our school? (to use when discussing history or literature)

There are several stumbling blocks one can encounter when implementing a teaching style based on open-ended questions. First, despite all your efforts, some students will be determined to give what they think are the right answers. When discussing bullying, these students often propose common and sometimes unrealistic adult advice—for example, that targets just walk away. When I believe students are parroting adult recommendations, I thank them and ask them about situations when they have used the proposed solution. If they have used the solution, I ask them how it worked. Often they have not used the given solution, and in these cases I ask them why not. I then encourage students to develop alternatives.

Other students will seem driven to give what they think are the wrong answers. It is likely that they are testing adults in front of their peers to see if adults do have a list of right answers beneath their open-ended questions. Often I respond by thanking students for their input and asking the rest of the class what effect the suggested solution would have. When students present a solution that I do not believe will work, I have found it most effective to encourage young people to evaluate the solution, basing it on their own experiences, rather than to veto it myself. Adults should veto only solutions that are not allowed at school, put students at risk, or do harm. Even in these situations, we should ask students what effect they think the given solution would have in order to help them see for themselves why the solution is unacceptable.

I have found that students derive many harmful solutions to social problems from television and movies. When we point out the distinctions between television or movies and real life, we help students see the real consequences of these behaviors. For example, we might ask young people to tell us what happens on television when someone teases or punches someone else and compare that to what happens in real life. We might ask about the difference between reactions to name-calling on television—where a laugh track teaches us that the name-calling is funny—and name-calling in real life.

Another potential problem when leading question-based interventions is the natural outspokenness or shyness of different individuals in a class or group. Some students will be more comfortable raising their hands and speaking out than others. Some students will need time to formulate their thoughts and may struggle to be heard. Since all students' opinions add constructively to a brainstorming session, staff leading discussions should make an effort to involve everybody. To achieve this, we can make our questions both open-ended and specific so that we can ask any student for an opinion. When we don't know the students, we can ask them to wear name tags so we can ask questions of individuals by name instead of asking the group as a whole. When students choose not to answer a question, I encourage them to say, "Please come back to me," instead of "I pass." I then return to them after hearing two other students' answers. When we ask specific questions of individuals, we can help ensure that students stay engaged and all opinions are equally valued.

Structuring Adequate Practice for Students to Reach Mastery

When we teach skills, it is crucial to structure sufficient time for practice, feedback, reteaching, and more practice. Only when students demonstrate mastery of a given skill over time should we move on to other skills. We should be careful not to underestimate the amount of time it can take for students to learn and internalize the simplest of skills. To prepare for the variability of real life, students should have the opportunity to practice skills in a variety of scenarios and settings. For example, when teaching playground behavior, we should practice both in the classroom and on the playground. When giving feedback, we should first focus on specific, effective actions and their positive results. Adults can also point out ineffective solutions and encourage students to make adjustments.

Improvisational theater allows students a safe environment in which to practice behaviors. Clear standards to ensure emotional safety and a question-based approach are both essential to this technique, which I often call skill practice. Guidelines should be set before the class period and should address how classmates are allowed to respond if someone does something silly on stage, stumbles over a line, or drops something. In the same way that we would not allow students to laugh at someone who makes a mistake in math class, we must set limits to prevent teasing. I explain these standards by emphasizing that there are no mistakes in theater, and any event on stage can be a springboard to creating a better scene.

We can help students become more comfortable with the idea of theater by stressing that they are already experts in improvisational acting. Every day, they wake up and confront situations in which they have no script. They choose words and actions all day long as they react to unpredictable situations. Improvisational theater training exercises can also help students warm up to acting. Exercises such as those in Koppett's 2001 book *Training to Imagine,* are similar to stretching before a sports game or practice. We can explain that just as physical stretches help us run faster, jump higher, and be more flexible, theater exercises help us imagine, create, and experiment more fully on stage. One exercise from Koppett's book illustrates the value of these techniques. In it, three students play the roles of news reporters interviewing a fourth student. The young person being interviewed plays the role of the world's leading expert on some complex topic. The expert is directed to make up answers to each question the reporters ask. This exercise often starts out a bit stiffly, but students begin to loosen up and be more creative when the actors realize that they can ask outlandish questions and give outlandish answers. For the second phase of Koppett's exercise, we enlist new student actors and assign the roles described above as well as one additional role. In this phase, the expert speaks only gibberish and the added actor plays the role of the interpreter. The reporters direct their questions to the interpreter, who translates the English questions into gibberish. The expert pretends not to understand the question until it is interpreted and then answers in gibberish. The interpreter then answers the reporters' questions. Students often loosen up and have fun with this exercise, especially when we encourage experts to give one-word answers, which the interpreters translate as very long answers. (Alternatively, experts can speak at length in gibberish, and the interpreter can translate their answers as "Yes.") Improvisational theater warm-ups help students approach problem-solving lessons with more creativity.

We can transition from theater exercises to social problem solving skill practice by first identifying a problem to explore. We randomly choose volunteers from the audience, and they act out the problem over and over again with different solutions. Throughout the improvisational process, we should ask open-ended questions such as "Did the solution work?" "Is there a better way to solve this problem?" "Would a different tone of voice help?" "What about different words?" and "What did we just learn?" For the student actors and the audience as a whole, solutions to social problems become more real and concrete through practice. With practice, it also becomes easier to distinguish between realistic and unrealistic solutions. The adult's role in these activities is to ask questions that challenge students to see and practice many solutions, help students assess these varying solutions, and remind students later of the list of solutions they came up with.

Providing Opportunities for Students to Teach Others

We deepen students' learning when we empower students to teach one another. Many people of all ages have told me that teaching others helps them internalize understanding. I have found that students take their learning more seriously when they accept the responsibility of teaching others. Students can teach others by making and displaying posters, presenting at assemblies, writing short articles for the parent newsletter, discussing their ideas with cross-grade reading buddies, and creating short instructional videos. While we encourage these interactions, we should work closely with students to focus their lessons on specific actions instead of letting them make vague statements, such as "No bullying allowed."

It is imperative that the messages students teach and the techniques they employ are their own. After the second-grade lesson on problem solving, previously discussed in this chapter, the second graders were excited by the idea of teaching older students as well as younger ones. We discussed different teaching techniques, and they decided on an instructional video and a series of posters illustrating their solutions.

Through newsletter articles, students can enlist their parents to follow up on lessons at home. Following is a recent example of a brief newsletter article:

What Makes Our School Special

When asked by Mr. Davis, our guidance counselor, what makes our school special, Ms. Fortin's fourth-grade class said:

1. We are all friends and classmates here—not enemies. We are all connected like a web.

2. We take the time to talk about what is important and how we do things at our school, like during Peace Day assemblies.

3. We introduce new people and make them feel welcome.

4. The whole school works together to encourage people.

5. You don't have to be in the same grade as someone else to be his or her friend.

6. We are all different, which is a great thing.

7. We make work a challenge instead of a chore.

Newsletter articles and parent discussions about bullying can help raise awareness and assist parents as they support their children and help them implement effective interventions when witnessing hitting, name-calling, or exclusion. When we work together with parents to build community consensus about what students should do when they see their peers hurting or excluding others, systemic and long-lasting change become more likely.

Following Up to Assess Implementation and Refine Solutions

Following up any lesson is essential if we want students to remember and implement the solutions they have formulated. This process starts during instruction. We can ask students to describe real situations in which they will be able to use the skills being developed. During and after any series of lessons, we should periodically ask students to describe a time when they used or could have used the solutions they generated and how the solutions worked. One way to do this is to list their solutions on the board and record how many students used each solution in the recent past. We can then ask students to rate the effectiveness of each solution on a scale of 1 to 5 and record the average ratings. This provides the opportunity to praise the use of effective solutions and fine-tune ineffective and unused solutions. In addition, when students recognize that a solution can be effective in one situation and ineffective in another, they realize that different situations and individuals require different solutions. Students may need more practice to feel comfortable using certain solutions, and we can encourage students to fine-tune not only their words, but also their tone of voice and body language.

When we create a space for students to reflect on their successes and how they achieved success, young people become more likely to repeat effective actions in the future. There are several factors involved in this trend. First, encouraging students to reflect honestly on their behavior helps them take ownership of their successes instead of attributing them to someone else or to luck. Seeing their successes also provides young people with the self-confidence to continue to strive toward further success, even if this requires taking risks and developing new solutions.

For the second-grade lesson on problem solving, described previously, my first follow-up activity was to post students' list of solutions on the board and talk about times they used the solutions in the previous week. I then asked them to brainstorm new problems not previously discussed. For each new problem, the students chose two solutions from their list. We tested these solutions with improvisational theater. When a solution did not work, we went back to the board to revise the solution or chose a different solution for the particular problem. I continued to follow up weekly with similar classroom activities, as well as informally in the halls and on the playground.

One of the most important follow-up techniques is to cue students in the moment and provide positive and corrective feedback. Toward this end, we should ensure that others on the school staff know about the solutions students generate so staff can prompt students to use their solutions and praise them when they are successful. Most effective are concrete statements, such as "When Tajandra wouldn't play with you today, you chose to play with someone else instead of fighting with her. It looked like you had fun" or "You sat with Ari when he was alone. Afterward, he was smiling." When we show students their own choices and the positive effects of those choices, we reinforce cause-and-effect thinking and students' awareness of their many options in every situation they encounter. We can also give feedback and invite reflection when students make choices that negatively affect themselves or others. In debriefing with students, we can ask, "What was the problem?" "What was your goal?" "What did you do?" "What happened when you did that?" and "What else could you do next time?" When adults use the language of problems, choices, and outcomes, instead of rules and consequences or adults' own emotions, young people are more likely to change their behavior. We model for students a specific type of feedback, which they can learn to give themselves. Over time, the set of solutions students develop can become part of the shared language and social norms of the school.

My colleagues and I at the Bean school have developed a structured process to encourage students to reflect on positive classroom and recess behavior. When students come in from recess, we ask them, "Did you have a fun recess?" When they answer in the affirmative, we ask them, "What did you do to make it a fun recess?" When students reply that they did not have a fun recess, we ask them what went wrong, what they could do next time to improve recess, and what adults could do to help them. This same process can be used in the classroom.

Staff can ask students at the beginning of the day to describe what kind of day they want to have and how they plan to achieve their goals. When staff write this list of planned actions on the board, they can refer back to the list throughout the day. At the end of the day, students can reflect on what kind of day they wanted, how they planned to meet their goals, what they actually did, and how they feel about the day.

On an even larger scale, we have implemented this technique during yearlong discussions. One of these discussions involved a class that had significant difficulties getting along at the beginning of the year. At the beginning of the school year and at several points along the way, we discussed the kind of classroom climate students wanted, what students could do to achieve this climate, and which solutions did and did not work. At the end of a year, during which time staff and students worked hard to improve the climate of the classroom, I asked the students, "What has changed in your classroom this year?" They answered that they got in trouble less and that criticism, arguing, name-calling, and interrupting had all decreased. They also told me that there was more kindness, constructive criticism, and inclusion. Next I asked them, "How did you achieve these changes?" Their responses varied, ranging from "We didn't spread rumors" to "We moved away from arguments instead of being pulled into them." At the beginning of the following school year, we reviewed our discussions from the previous year. Students again described the changes they enacted and how they achieved change. They also set additional goals for the upcoming year, and we continue to discuss and evaluate.

BUILDING SKILLS SPECIFIC TO BYSTANDER SCENARIOS

The teaching techniques outlined thus far in this chapter begin to encourage bystanders of bullying to take positive and effective action. Lodge and Frydenberg (2005) found that students with altruistic feelings and effective problem-solving and coping skills were more likely to support targets of bullying than students without these skills. We can continue to build on the work of teaching empathy and social problem solving skills by focusing on specific bystander interventions. We can structure a series of classroom meetings using open-ended questions to focus on peer aggression and bystander action. The following lesson sequence illustrates.

Session 1

During the first session, we discuss the types of bystander situations young people and adults experience, focusing on three categories: directly seeing one person's being cruel to another, becoming aware that friends are fighting with each other, and observing peers who are socially isolated. We can help students understand that both young people and adults are regularly exposed to all three of these situations.

Sessions 2–3

During the second and third sessions, we can start by asking students what adults typically do, or should do, when presented with the first category of bystander scenarios. We can ask what adults could and should do when they see someone yell at a child in the supermarket, use racist language, or commit a crime. We move on to discuss and practice possible actions for students to take when they observe peers acting cruelly toward others. As we continue to ask open-ended questions and encourage students to develop many possible solutions, we can use the brainstormed list of adult bystander actions as a guide. In order to master effective solutions, we can use improvisational theater to test solutions specific to bystanders.

Session 4

During the fourth session, we can discuss what students in the class *have* done in bystander situations since the first session. We can help students evaluate the success of each bystander intervention on the basis of its safety for the bystander and effectiveness in supporting the target.

Sessions 5–7

During sessions 5–7, we can follow the same sequence of questions as in sessions 2–4, but this time focus on what adults and peer bystanders can do when friends fight. Again, we can start by asking students what adults do, or should do, when a couple they know breaks up or when two of their friends argue. From this discussion, we can transition to asking students what they can do when they see friends fight and what they have done in these scenarios. A sample lesson focusing on helping students develop and implement effective bystander interventions for relational aggression can be found in Appendix C.

Sessions 8–10

During sessions 8–10, we can follow the same pattern of questions but instead focus on what adults and peer bystanders can do when they become aware that someone is socially isolated in the workplace, community, or school.

At the end of these 10 sessions, young people will have generated a set of skills they can use in a wide range of bystander situations. By focusing on open-ended questions, we help students take ownership and thus increase the possibility that they will use the skills generated.

Following is a list of positive bystander actions created by a fourth-grade class at the Bean school:

- Don't make things worse by laughing or joining in.
- Tell an adult.
- Help targets get away from the bullying.
- Be a friend to targets by sitting with them, playing with them, and showing them that the bullying is not their fault.
- If a friend or a younger student is bullying, ask the individual to stop in a peaceful way.

To fine-tune student-created solutions, we can discuss their effectiveness and experiment with modifications in words, tone of voice, and body language. We should frequently follow up our discussions of bystander action by praising effective solutions and revising ineffective solutions.

Different Situations, Different Responses

We should remember that not all bystander situations are the same. It is crucial for students to receive specific, explicit messages about their responsibilities as bystanders and their expected responses when faced with real or potential aggression. Stueve et al. (2006) propose that we involve parents, staff, and students in differentiating types of bystander situations and identifying appropriate responses for each type. When we ask students to think about effective responses to different bystander situations, we help them see that solutions vary depending on the severity of situations. Students should learn to deal differently with potential school violence, hitting, name-calling, rumors, exclusion, cyberbullying, and relational aggression.

Relational Aggression

When discussing differentiated responses to peer-to-peer aggression, we can address relational aggression and brainstorm bystander actions specific to this form of bullying. Relational aggression, or bullying within friendships, is common among all students in all age groups, though some research indicates that it is most common among girls in late elementary school and middle school. Much like domestic abuse, relational aggression is complicated by bonds of friendship and is often characterized by an unequal power dynamic, manipulation, and a cycle of aggressive behavior and "making up." Friendship may be presented conditionally. This type of bullying is often underhanded and subtle, though targets can attest to the deep hurt caused by seemingly minor offenses. Mullin writes, "Relational aggression may be particularly insidious because victims often allow themselves to be subjected to these acts in silence—often out of a combined desire to fit in and fear of further ostracism" (2003, p. 9). I have observed similar patterns of behavior between third-grade girls and between teenage girls and their verbally and physically abusive boyfriends. I worry that if girls label hurtful relationships "friendships" in childhood, they may be more likely to label abusive relationships "love" later in life.

When discussing relational aggression, we can focus on helping targets leave painful friendships while helping bystanders support targets by maintaining friendships with both parties and refusing to take a role in aggressive behavior, teasing, or manipulation. As I will discuss in more detail in chapter 5, we can start teaching students as young as four or five how to avoid being controlled by their peers. At the Bean school, we have found that after repeatedly teaching and practicing nonconfrontational techniques for refusing to go along with controlling friends, students attempt to control others much less often. When young people don't gain popularity and power by exhibiting controlling behaviors, they become less likely to exhibit those behaviors.

Merely encouraging targets to leave abusive friendships is not enough, just as focusing our domestic violence interventions solely on encouraging targets to leave their abusive partners is not sufficient. We should also address the actions bystanders can take to worsen or improve situations of relational aggression. In the following scenario, Wellman shows how aggressors often enlist others to hurt their targets:

> Someone is mad at Kelly and tries to get all Kelly's friends mad at her, too. This is called "alliance building." Without ever confronting Kelly with her grievance, this "friend" sets it up for Kelly to be excluded from the lunch table, ignored in the halls, and not invited to the weekend sleepover. In this scenario, girls need help in identifying the roles of aggressor, victim, and girls in the middle. They need to know that this kind of alliance building is a form of bullying. They need to know that this is as harmful as taking Kelly behind the school and beating her up. (2002, para. 14)

Wellman makes a subtle but important shift in language to describing bystanders as "girls in the middle." This shift emphasizes the complexity of relational aggression and the many roles students take to maintain, intensify, or diminish hurtful behavior and manipulation. In discussions with students, we can strive to help them understand the complex dynamics of relational aggression and see that they can inadvertently hurt others by taking sides or going along with an aggressive friend. After discussing the negative impact and dynamics of relational aggression, I ask students what actions make the situation worse or better. Young people reply that taking sides and making up or spreading rumors makes the situation worse.

They tell me that in relation to cyberbullying—using the Internet and other electronic means to engage in bullying behavior—students take hurtful roles by disseminating user names, passwords, and other information. Students report that maintaining friendships with both parties and refusing to spread rumors or exclude targets improves the situation.

Resisting the temptation to spread gossip, exclude targets, or otherwise get involved can be difficult, especially because, as Mullin (2003) points out, the students involved are often motivated by a desire to fit into the popular group. When popularity is emphasized within a group of students, it becomes easier for popular students to abuse their power and enlist others to help them bully. When the school culture shifts and students no longer allow an elite group to hold all the power, it becomes easier for students in the middle to refuse to go along with bullying without fear of being ostracized.

One year at the Bean school, the fifth grade decided that one of their goals for the year was to prevent a popular group from gaining power. When I asked them what specific actions they could take to achieve this goal, they replied that they could consciously avoid being impressed when their peers called themselves popular and refuse to play with peers who tried to manipulate and control them. During our monthly Peace Day assemblies, we discussed the successes and challenges of their goal. Due to their hard work and motivation, this fifth-grade class enjoyed a year free of the typical power struggles, tears, and fights about group membership. During the following year, after seeing a popular group emerge quickly, school staff told the new fifth graders about what the previous fifth grade had achieved. Students outside the new popular group built alliances and friendships based on inclusiveness and kindness, and popularity quickly receded as an issue.

Interventions to combat relational aggression thus often combine skill building and shifts in social norms. To delve deeper into ways to teach students about this type of bullying, please refer to the sample lesson described in detail in Appendix C, which focuses on helping bystanders avoid behaviors that escalate and worsen relational aggression.

SUMMARY AND CONCLUSIONS

In the end, building empathy and social problem solving skills is an unpredictable process of discovery. Facilitators of this process should simultaneously have teaching objectives in mind and be open and flexible to allow students to direct their own learning. Success in this process comes when we use a question-based approach, provide time and space for brainstorming and practice, and follow up our lessons both formally and informally. Teaching students to solve social problems can change the culture of the school so that social norms are to seek out and implement effective solutions to small problems, alert adults to big problems, and intervene effectively during and after bullying situations.

Chapter 4

A Sample Skills-Based Workshop for Bystanders

In order to illustrate many of the teaching techniques described in the previous chapter, I will describe in detail a one-day workshop I presented for a group of 45 seventh graders in 2004. The students who participated in the workshop chose to do so because they wanted to shift from passively watching bullying to actively defending targets. I explain these workshop procedures to provide concrete examples of ways to raise awareness about bullying and teach social problem solving skills through open-ended questions and practice, and to help you lead your own discussions. Every presenter possesses his or her own style, and every discussion will be unique. I offer the following detailed example as only a rough guide, one I hope you will adapt to your own style and the needs of your students. It is important to remember that one-day workshops for students are unlikely to be effective unless they accompany a schoolwide, staff-led bullying prevention program, as this workshop did. In addition, ongoing skills training is most effective when led by school staff who later can prompt students in the moment, instead of by outsiders like myself.

QUESTIONS AND AN INTRODUCTION

I start the presentation with several questions to determine what the students know and where they stand. I ask them why they think I choose to present this workshop for bystanders instead of for youth who bully or youth who are bullied. Students reply that, unlike bullies, bystanders often want to reduce bullying and, unlike targets, they may have the power to do so. I ask them what they like about their school and community. They talk about their favorite teachers, friends, and hobbies. Some of them talk about feeling safer in this school than in other schools they have attended. They tell me about their principal, who "won't let kids be mean here."

I then introduce myself and explain my background, asking questions as I go. I ask them why they think I saw more targets than bullies in private therapy. A girl in the second row answers that targets need help to change bullying behavior, while bullies choose the behavior and can choose to stop. I talk about my work preventing bullying in schools and how I've come to work primarily with staff and bystanders because these two groups define what behaviors are acceptable and unacceptable, who gets peer approval, and who is left out. I talk about my work during the civil rights movement and with victims of domestic abuse, sexual harassment, and child abuse. I tell the students that from all of these experiences I have learned that supportive communities build safety and encourage healing for targets of abuse and harassment.

During other workshops, I have talked about different aspects of my background, including the anti-Semitic harassment I experienced as a Jew growing up in Boston in the 1950s, what I learned working at rape crisis centers, and what I learned from talking with young people who are bullied. I have found it effective to begin any workshop with a brief personal introduction to establish who I am and why I do what I do. The often-quoted saying "They don't care how much you know until they know how much you care" applies especially to any workshop with students who don't already know the presenter. Balanced against the need to share ourselves with students is the necessity of keeping this part of our workshop brief so students stay engaged. Keeping this balance in mind, we can choose elements of our personal stories that establish our personal commitment to social justice and help students begin to think about the broader issues that surround and inform bullying prevention work.

I notice during the introduction that two boys and one girl begin to raise their hands frequently and answer nearly all of the questions. I know that if I let this happen, others will disengage. Because I have learned that this pattern often emerges, I have arranged for all the students to wear name tags so I can address them individually. For the remainder of the workshop, I wander through the audience, asking specific questions of individuals. As a wider variety of students express themselves, the conversation becomes deeper and more meaningful. I thank the frequent contributors for their thoughts and explain to them that I want to hear from everybody.

I tell the audience that I often stage a bullying scene to begin my workshops. Before the workshop, I enlist two students to sit in front and instruct one to make fun of the other. I tell them in advance to continue this behavior even after I rebuke them. I ask the audience how they think groups react to this simulation. Instead of answering this question, as most groups do, these students answer another question: "Why do audiences rarely react?" They tell me that because adults are present, students assume that the adults will take care of the situation if it is a problem. I acknowledge and affirm their thoughts and ask my initial question again: "What do they think audiences do during this situation?" Eventually, one student in the audience says that silence and laughter are the likeliest reactions. I ask them if silence and laughter are also frequent reactions to bullying in real life, and they say that they are. I ask how silence and laughter affect bullies and targets. They tell me that silence and laughter encourage bullies to continue their behavior and teach targets that they deserve to be bullied.

I return to this theme throughout the presentation by making the audience laugh as I play the role of a bully during interactive theater scenes, then pointing out how easy it is to make them laugh. I ask them each time how their laughter affects my character, and they tell me that it encourages bullying. After several repetitions of this pattern, they stop laughing. I point out the change and encourage them to continue it in their day-to-day lives.

A VIDEO EXAMPLE

My next step is to show an excerpt from the video *Let's Get Real* (Chasnoff, 2004), during which a teenage girl describes her reaction to having a male peer grab her buttocks against her will.

I ask the students, "What kind of aggression is this?"

They answer, "Sexual harassment."

"Will she tell anyone?" I ask.

Most students say that she probably won't.

"Why not?" I ask.

"She is embarrassed," students tell me.

"She is afraid others will make fun of her."

"She is afraid of rumors being spread about her."

"She is afraid of not being protected from retaliation for telling."

"She is afraid of not being taken seriously and criticized for bringing the harassment on herself."

"She is afraid of being told that she should like what he did and like him."

"If she tells, who will she tell?" I ask.

The audience answers, "Friends" and "Parents."

Then I ask, "What might her friends do?"

"They might make things worse, and then she wouldn't tell again," they answer.

"They might help."

"What could her friends do to shut her down and make sure she doesn't tell again?" I ask.

"They could make light of the situation," students answer.

"They could spread rumors about her as someone who flirts or tell her it's no big deal."

"They could tell her the boy likes her and she should like him."

"They could tell her the boy is hot and ask her if she is some kind of lesbian who doesn't like boys."

"They could go to teachers without asking her and involve them before she's ready."

I ask what peers could do to improve the situation.

Students answer, "Tell her it's not her fault."

"Go to a teacher together."

"Not spread rumors or blame her."

We watch the next segment of the video to see what the girl's friend actually does, which is to go with her to a teacher to minimize her embarrassment. The students agree that this action is positive.

I stop the video again and ask the group, "What could the teacher do to make the situation worse?"

They answer, "He could be too busy to listen."

"She could say that boys will be boys and girls should put up with their behavior in order to get a boyfriend."

"He could sit down with the girl and the boy together and try to work things out."

In response to this last comment I draw a parallel to being mugged. After being mugged, I would not want to sit down with my attacker and try to work things out.

"What could the teacher do to make things better?" I ask.

"She could keep her eyes open."

"He could make sure it doesn't happen again."

We watch the next segment of the video to see what the teacher actually does, which is to listen calmly, thank the girl for telling, and stop the boy from doing it again by keeping the boy away from her.

At the end of this video, the girl says, "They made him stay with the boys and stay away from the girls. So it's really good [to tell]—because if you keep it to yourself nothing is going to change and it's never going to stop."

It is clear to the audience that the girl's friend and teacher responded in ways that made her feel safe and empowered.

My last question for the students to think about is this: "How can you be good friends in a situation like this?"

The students talk about listening supportively, walking with targets, reassuring targets that it's not their fault, discouraging rumors by not spreading them, and going with targets to adults to ask for help.

MAGIC AND A POEM

Next, I transition into a magic routine called What Is Bullying? which I describe in more detail in Appendix F. This effect begins as a puppet show about power imbalances and evolves into a historical review of attitudes surrounding bullying.

We take a 10-minute break, and on return I tell the students about my background as a Jew who lost family members in the Holocaust. I combine magic and storytelling to illustrate the historical impact of bystanders' choices to act or be silent. I use a magic effect based on the work of minister and magician Robert Neale (1991) that illustrates Pastor Martin Niemöller's often-quoted passage, written in reference to the Holocaust. This passage—often presented as a poem—has been adapted by many groups and exists in many variations. The version of Niemöller's passage on the facing page appears in an inscription at the New England Holocaust Memorial in Boston, Massachusetts.

IMPROVISATIONAL THEATER

We move next into improvisational theater. I act as the bully, one student acts as the target, and three students take on the roles of bystanders. I make fun of the target's hair and clothes and then ask the audience how they think the target feels. They answer, "sad," "angry," and "hurt." As I continue to ask how the target might be feeling, someone points out that the target probably feels lonely. I ask why. Audience members point out that the target feels lonely because no one is doing anything to help, and thus the target may believe that everyone agrees with the bully.

As often happens, someone says the target may feel embarrassed, which provides an opportunity to discuss injustice. I ask who in the scene has done something wrong. They point to me as the bully.

"Who," I ask, "is feeling embarrassed?"

They point to the target. I ask them if this is fair. They reply that it is not. They tell me the bully should feel embarrassed, and the target, who did nothing wrong, has no reason to feel embarrassed.

Sometimes at this point in the discussion, students state that the target has done something wrong by not standing up to or fighting back against the bully. When I hear this statement, I ask

They came first for the Communists,

And I didn't speak up because I wasn't a Communist.

Then they came for the Jews,

And I didn't speak up because I wasn't a Jew.

Then they came for the trade unionists,

And I didn't speak up because I wasn't a trade unionist.

Then they came for the Catholics,

And I didn't speak up because I was a Protestant.

Then they came for me,

And by that time no one was left to speak up.

—Martin Niemöller

about the target's options for action. We might act out each option in order to recognize the improbability that the target's actions will improve the bullying situation and the very real chance that action by the target would lead to more damaging retaliation from the bully. Through this process of inquiry and acting, students usually come to the same conclusion as Dr. Jodie Lodge: that targets who fight back are more likely to continue to be bullied than those who do not (University of Melbourne, 2006).

I then ask the audience what bystanders can do to help. The students' first answer, as in the vast majority of more than 500 workshops I have led over the past eight years, is for bystanders to intervene directly by telling the bully to stop. To illustrate the difficulty of this solution, I draw a parallel to what they should or would do if they saw a convenience store being robbed: "I certainly wouldn't go inside and tell the robber to stop," I state. (I admit that I used to advise bystanders to stand up directly to bullies until I realized I was asking them to take too much of a risk.)

After discarding confrontation as a possible solution, I ask the audience what else bystanders can do to help targets.

"They can help the target get away," one student suggests.

"Okay. Why doesn't the target just walk away alone?" I ask, digging deeper.

Students answer, "Walking away brands targets as vulnerable, and bullies could follow them."

"Walking away is rude." In other words, it contradicts polite standards that tell us not to walk away when someone is talking to us.

"It feels unsafe and weak to walk away, as if targets are admitting defeat."

"Why is it important, then, for bystanders to invite targets to walk away with them?" I ask.

"Because that way targets can get away without feeling weak."

"How can we help targets get away?" I ask, probing for specific and realistic solutions.

We discuss and agree that the best strategy would be to stay at a distance and make up an excuse to help the target get away. Again we act out a bullying scenario, this time with different student actors, and again I make fun of the target.

Even after our discussion, the bystanders continue to watch the bullying silently. When I ask them why they don't practice the intervention we just discussed, they say it is hard and scary to interrupt. I tell them that this is why they are here today—to practice. I say, "Just like when you play sports, if you don't practice you don't perform well in the real world."

We repeat the scene three more times before the bystanders interrupt me. The target is clearly grateful as he walks away with them.

I choose new actors from the audience and ask, "What else can bystanders do to help targets?" Students reply that they could get a teacher or befriend the target. We practice these solutions until the students seem comfortable with them.

ROLE PLAY: INTERVENING IN INDIRECT HARASSMENT

I transition to the next phase of the workshop by performing a magic routine called Finding a Good Friend, described in more detail in Appendix F. The goal of this routine is to show how including isolated peers benefits everyone involved. I move into this effect by reminding the students that they identified loneliness as an effect of being bullied. I tell them, and check for agreement, that teens consistently identify social isolation as the most painful aspect of being bullied.

Next, I ask students to describe bullying scenarios they have observed in their school, without using names. I write the list on an easel pad. I split the students randomly into three groups and, after a few of Koppett's (2001) theater exercises, I ask them to choose three scenarios to act out in their small groups. I tell them to brainstorm and practice three solutions to each scenario and choose one scenario to present to the larger group. Teachers supervise each group as I circulate.

When we come back together 45 minutes later, we watch the first scene. In this scenario, several students use the words *gay* and *queer* as all-purpose insults. They use the terms as negative adjectives to describe clothes, movies, and school tests. They also call other students gay in an insulting manner. Students demonstrate three bystander solutions: helping targets get away, changing the subject, and telling adults what they see and hear.

I show the students a poster of the Pyramid of Hate (Anti-Defamation League, 2000). I use this graphic to illustrate how indirect harassment can lead to serious prejudice, discrimination, and violence. I tell the audience that indirect harassment makes bigots feel supported in their prejudice and justified to commit verbal or physical harassment.

I next ask the audience whom the following statement hurts: "That test is so gay." Their first response is that the statement hurts the teacher who created the test. I ask the teachers present if they are upset when students don't like their tests, and the answer is a resounding "No." As I continue to push students to examine whom these statements really hurt, audience members state that they can make gay or questioning youth feel unsafe.

We talk about the comment "The team played like girls." The girls in the audience report that when they hear statements like this, they begin to believe that girls can't play well, which in turn encourages them not to try.

As a personal example, I talk about the fear I feel when I hear anti-Semitic jokes. A girl in the front row asks with startled concern, "Why would that make you afraid?" I answer that anti-

Semitic joking makes me think about the murder and persecution of Jews during the Holocaust and in other eras. I explain that ethnic genocide is only possible when prejudice goes unchallenged and thus leads to hatred and fear.

We end this conversation by practicing and discussing additional ways students can respond when they hear indirect harassment. In this situation, I allow students to include direct confrontation in their list of possible solutions because kindly telling a friend to stop is often an effective solution for curbing indirect harassment.

ROLE PLAY: RESPONDING TO RUMORS

The second group presents a skit focusing on rumors. One student plays the role of someone who learns embarrassing information about a classmate and tells others, who in turn tell more students. The group demonstrates several solutions: changing the subject, walking away when they hear the rumor, and telling the person spreading the rumor to stop. I tell them about my experience working with students at the Bean school on the issue of rumors. During a fifth-grade unit about rumors, we talked about many actions students could take to minimize the spread of rumors, including directly telling their friends and classmates to stop. When I followed up with these students a month later, they told me that rumors continued to spread. When I asked why they weren't using the solutions we discussed previously, they told me they didn't want to confront their friends and risk retaliation. They told me they had forgotten the nonconfrontational solutions we discussed. During this follow-up conversation, we discarded confrontation as a potential solution and practiced nonconfrontational ways to react to rumors. Among other solutions, the Bean school students practiced changing the subject, appearing interested and then not passing on the rumor, and befriending the target of the rumor. During a second follow-up conversation, students told me of their success. Discarding direct confrontation allowed them to implement more realistic solutions.

After describing my experience at the Bean school, I ask the students attending the workshop to create and practice a variety of techniques to distract from, defuse, and avoid spreading rumors without confrontation. They practice the same scene three times, each time with a different bystander action: changing the subject, inviting the person starting the rumor to play a game instead of continuing the discussion, and nodding but not spreading the rumor to anyone else.

ROLE PLAY: NAME-CALLING

The third group presents a skit about name-calling. In this scenario, one student calls another names about his appearance, intelligence, and family. In the beginning, bystanders watch in silence; afterward, they demonstrate several possible solutions. As a group, we discuss what the body language and facial expressions of the actors tell us about how they feel. I then encourage the audience to brainstorm additional bystander solutions. The actors playing the roles of bystanders experiment with each technique as they replay the scene over and over again. Their solutions include helping the youth being bullied get away, distracting the student who is bullying, telling an adult, and spending time with the target later. One student suggests asking one of the bully's close friends to have a talk with the bully, and we practice this scenario with an additional actor drawn from the audience.

SUMMARY AND CONCLUSIONS

We summarize the three groups' skits by reviewing the solutions they developed and grouping them into four categories: being an honest witness, standing with the target during and after incidents of bullying, distracting the bully and helping the target get away, and telling friends to cut it out in an affectionate and direct manner.

I end with a magic routine focused on the idea that small actions can lead to big effects. During this effect, described in detail in Appendix F, I blow bubbles while reciting Mahatma Gandhi's statement "Whatever you do will be insignificant, but it is very important that you do it." I refer to behaviors and actions they created and tested in their skits. I say, "These small actions make a real and durable difference," as I transform the last bubble I blow into a large glass marble. I hold the marble gently as though still holding a bubble before dropping it on the table, where it lands loudly without breaking. When the uproar created by this final effect dies down, I lift the marble and end by asking the students the following three questions:

"Did you have a good time?"

They answer, "Yes."

"Did you learn something?"

"Yes."

"Are you going to DO something to stop bullying?"

"YES!" they shout.

Immediately after the workshop, students write me letters listing the solutions and actions they plan to use in bystander situations and asking me questions. I reply with a group letter summarizing what the students told me, reinforcing the power of the actions they have chosen, and answering their questions.

I discuss further follow-up with the principal and teachers. We plan for staff to cue students to use the behaviors they learned, praise students when they use effective solutions, provide ongoing practice opportunities, and help the students see the positive effects of their actions.

Chapter 5

Shared Language, Social Norms, and School Climate

If a student feels that bullying is "part of growing up" or "'harm-less," he or she is less likely to feel upset when bullying or observing others being bullied. Indeed, a positive attitude toward aggression is highly associated with the propensity to bully others. . . . Whereas this is not a surprising finding, it suggests a need to iden-tify environmental factors that foster a proviolence attitude in schools.

—*Espelage and Swearer (2003)*

POSITIVE EFFECTS OF SCHOOL CLIMATE INTERVENTIONS

Denise Koebcke, a bullying prevention program coordinator in Indiana, told me the following story about the effects of school climate interventions (personal communication, October 23, 2006). For over a decade, two teachers in her school district taught a Holocaust unit to eighth graders in several area schools. The unit relies on a simulation designed to help students understand how humans can be cruel to one another. During the simulation, students who are winning a game are given more and more power over those who are losing. Teachers noticed that each year the winners predictably became more vicious and aggressive as the simulation progressed. At the peak of the cruelty, the teachers ended the simulation to point out how power can corrupt and ultimately lead to atrocities such as the Holocaust.

Starting in 2003, Koebcke implemented middle school bystander discussion groups in response to rampant relational aggression. She expanded these groups into bystander leadership groups for eighth graders, who met weekly to discuss current issues and model inclusive, prosocial behavior at school and beyond. This program created a solid core of peer leaders who were held accountable for creating a more positive social climate among their peers. Koebcke continued her intervention by coordinating the implementation of a K–12 bullying prevention program based on the Ophelia Project's Creating a Safe School model, which aims to change social norms in the school community through staff and parent involvement, peer mentoring, and creating a common language surrounding aggression schoolwide (Ophelia Project, n.d.).

In 2005, teachers found that eighth graders at both middle schools where Koebcke implemented the bullying prevention program became much less vicious and aggressive during the simulation than they had been in previous years. Students simply refused to take the simulation to the past level of nastiness. At the end of the unit, the teachers were proud to report that the bullying prevention program had ruined their most powerful activity by changing the school's peer culture.

Another example of the potential impact of interventions to shift shared language, social norms, and school culture comes from the Bean school. Over years of conscious creation of a positive school culture, students at the school have developed a clear set of standards as to what types of language are and are not acceptable and allowed. One day, a fifth grader approached me on the playground to tell me that a new boy had said, "Girls are dumb." When I arrived at the scene, a group of boys and girls were already talking politely with the new boy. They acknowledged that such language might have been allowed at his old school but made it clear to him that this language was not acceptable at the Bean school. They requested my presence simply to reinforce their lesson. These students were able to stand up to the boy and tell him, "We don't say that here," because they recognized the potential negative impact of his statement and knew staff and other students would back them up. This is possible within a school culture that emphasizes mutual kindness and support.

School culture, which can be seen as an accumulation of social norms, is a major factor in determining how safe students feel and how they act in the face of injustice. These norms encompass schoolwide definitions of acceptable and unacceptable behavior, the language staff and students use, and the ways in which individuals handle conflict. Adults and students alike have the power to shift culture by consciously changing the way they think, talk, and act.

SHIFTS IN SHARED LANGUAGE

The first step in this process is to recognize subtle assumptions, typical behaviors, and the underlying messages hidden in commonly used language. Assumptions, behaviors, and language arise from many sources, including professional traditions and jargon, mass media, and schools' surrounding communities. When we recognize the current social norms in our schools, we can begin to shift toward shared norms and language that stress choices, justice, honesty, kindness, and inclusion. Empowering students to recognize and consciously change school norms engages young people in the process, thus making success more likely and showing students that they have the power to create a more just world. School staff possess the power to make a difference in the lives of young people by shifting social norms through role-modeling, teaching explicit lessons on these topics, and empowering students to take ownership of setting and achieving goals to improve school climate.

Consciously Choosing Language

Young people watch and listen to adults carefully. School staff, therefore, have a profound impact on students through their everyday words and actions. Adults can begin to shift social norms by questioning their own reactions to aggressive behavior and continue by consciously reshaping approaches schoolwide. One place to start is by examining adults' choice of language. When staff members choose language that emphasizes excuses and young people's inability to change their behavior, students learn these messages. When staff focus on the language of choices, cause-and-effect thinking, and ownership of emotions, they help young people understand the effects of their actions and reinforce the possibility of change.

The words we choose frequently imply unintended meanings, which shape and communicate social norms. This is true in the larger culture as well as in school culture. For example, think about the difference between "drunk-driving accident" and "drunk-driving crash." Describing a car crash as an accident removes responsibility from the driver. Also applying to the larger culture as well as to the school culture is the difference between advocating for "tolerance" of diversity and "celebration" of diversity. Individual differences are truly a reason for celebration and not something we should just tolerate. Communicating this idea through the language we choose can help all people feel accepted and valued.

We can choose to describe students as "bad kids" with "bad behavior," or we can state that students make "bad choices." The first two descriptions discount the possibility of change and make a value judgment about students as people. The third speaks in terms of choices, helps adults ally with young people, and communicates the possibility of change.

Adults help young people take responsibility for their actions and emotions when they shift from "because" to "when" or "after" as they describe student behavior. For example, there is a difference between saying, "Kelly hit Steve because he made faces at her" and "Kelly hit Steve after he made faces at her." The first statement implies that it is Steve's fault that Kelly decided to hit him. This statement minimizes the possibility that Kelly could have dealt with the situation in another way. The second statement emphasizes that Kelly had control over her actions and chose to hit Steve instead of choosing a more productive solution.

Along the same lines, we can discuss emotions with students by saying, "Tell me about a time when you got angry about something someone did" instead of "Tell me about a time when someone made you angry." The difference between these two statements is subtle but powerful. The first statement implies that we can choose whether to get angry or not, while the second statement implies that others control our emotions.

Our language can enable students' negative behaviors by providing them with excuses. When I visit schools, I often hear adults make statements such as "Katie had a hard time behaving in class." This statement implies that Katie does not have control over her behavior. Instead, we can concretely describe Katie's behaviors and point out the natural consequences of those behaviors. We can say, "Katie threw erasers at other students and stopped them from learning. As a result, she sat away from the other students for a while."

In addition, when disciplining students, staff can encourage students to take responsibility for their behaviors by saying, "You earned a detention," instead of "I'm giving you a detention." By clearly placing the responsibility for the detention on the shoulders of students, the first statement is more likely to lead to change as students strive to avoid future detentions. The second statement can encourage students to blame adults for their consequences.

Other common phrases used with young people include the ideas that they "need to," "should," or "must" follow the directions of an adult. This language can be confusing to young people. I remember hearing a teacher telling a group of rambunctious kindergarten students, "You need to settle down." The fact that the students were running around the room seemed to demonstrate the exact opposite—that what the students really needed was to be active. Instead of using the confusing statement "You need to settle down," adults can make a simple request, such as "Please sit down," or clearly and concretely point out to students the positive and negative consequences of their actions. We might say, "You have a choice. You may sit and work quietly, or you may sit away from the group. Which will you do?" We can also say, "When you sit down and listen, you get your work done" or "When you are kind to others, you make new friends."

It is important to remember that while it may seem harsh to hold students fully responsible for their behaviors, as long as we maintain a positive feeling tone, these statements communicate to students that it is their behavior that is unacceptable, not who they are as people. Many of these subtle shifts in language indicate a shift in perception from making excuses for actions to making choices that have consequences.

Following is a selection of examples of ways staff can shift their language. The bullying prevention committee at Melrose Veterans' Memorial Middle School in Melrose, Massachusetts, and I developed this list of language shifts to be implemented schoolwide.

Instead of saying . . .	Try saying . . .
"He/she is being bullied/ teased because . . ."	"He/she is being bullied/ teased about . . ."
"I feel . . ."	"I notice . . ."
"How would you feel if. . .?"	"How do you think he/she felt?" or "We don't allow that here."
"Stop tattling."	"Thank you for telling me."
"Nice job!"	"I noticed that you . . ."
"What happened?"	"What did you do?"
"Just ignore it" or "Work it out."	"What have you tried already?"
"Why did you do that?"	"We don't allow that here."
"You are a bully" or "You are bullying . . ."	"We don't allow that behavior here."

The final item in the Melrose list focuses on an important issue in choosing schoolwide language: to what extent we use the word *bullying* in day-to-day discussions and interventions. The word *bullying* has many different definitions. Some definitions require that aggressors intend to harm targets or cause distress. Intention is often impossible to prove because aggressive youth may be accomplished liars. Many definitions of bullying require that the behavior be repeated. However, when adults see aggressive behavior, they may not be aware of earlier incidents. In addition, this requirement may lead people to believe that single aggressive incidents are unimportant. Most definitions of bullying include the requirement that the aggressor have more power or status than the target. Yet the real power dynamics of a group of children or teens are subtle, ever-changing, and difficult for adults to understand fully. For these reasons, I believe we should describe specific, unacceptable actions concretely and say, "That behavior is not allowed here because it can hurt others," instead of "That is bullying."

The term *bullying* is sometimes also used to describe more serious or illegal behavior. If an action is actually assault, sexual or racial harassment, or another behavior prohibited by law, calling that action bullying can reduce our ability to change the aggressor's behavior and protect the target. When student behavior violates state or federal law, we should acknowledge that violation and act accordingly in cooperation with law enforcement authorities.

Teaching Schoolwide Shared Language

To further encourage change, adults can discuss language with young people and explicitly teach a schoolwide shared language. The following three classroom examples show how, through language-based interventions, school staff can contribute to a positive school culture that stresses effective solutions to social problems. You are likely to encounter opportunities to use similar techniques to discuss specific words and their meanings and thus help students develop positive behavior patterns.

Because . . .

I began a third-grade guidance lesson by sharing with the class an e-mail I received from a parent of a student at another school. The parent wrote, "I am concerned about the fairness of our school's discipline system. A student was disciplined for hitting, even though that hitting was caused by another student's teasing. The other student was disciplined, too, but this seems unfair to me. What do you think?" After asking the students what they thought, I wrote the word *because* on the board. I asked the class what they thought the word meant.

They replied, "It's the reason for something."

I nodded and wrote the following examples on the board:

- The ice cream melted because I left it out in the sun.
- The car stopped because it ran out of gas.
- I hit him because he hit me.
- I called my brother names because I was mad at him.

I asked the class if they saw a difference between the first two examples and the second two examples. They replied that there was a difference. When I asked what the difference was, one student stated, "Ice cream doesn't have any other options but to melt. People do have other options." Another student differentiated between statements by saying that the first two were examples of reasons and the second two were examples of excuses. I asked for more examples of sentences with *because* in them, and we placed these sentences in the two categories. I asked the students to explain what they had learned. When the teacher and I followed up with the students, we saw an increase in students' willingness to take responsibility for their behavior.

No Means No

The second example describes a guidance lesson with a kindergarten class. Before this lesson, I talked with the class about the importance of listening. This time, I began with a review of our previous lesson by asking, "What happens when you listen to people?"

The students answered, "You get more friends."

"What happens when you don't listen to people?" I asked.

"You get less friends," they answered.

At this point, I moved to my chosen topic for the day: the word *no*. "What does it mean when someone says no?" I asked.

"They want you to stop doing something," the kindergartners replied.

I asked for a volunteer to practice what to do when someone says no. I chose a student, and she proceeded to the front of the classroom. She and I faced each other so the rest of the class could see us.

I picked up a toy and said, "Let's pretend that this is a toy I brought from home. My grandmother gave it to me, and I want to keep it safe. You want to play with it, too. Ask me if you can play with it."

"Can I play with your toy?" the student helper asked.

"No," I replied. "My grandmother gave it to me." I paused and then asked the class, "What should she do next?"

"Ask again nicely," a boy from the audience replied.

I turned to the student helper and said, "You heard Ethan. Go ahead and ask again nicely."

"Please can I play with that?" she asked me in a kind way.

I replied, "No. My grandmother gave it to me," and then asked the class, "What should she do now?"

The class continued to suggest that the student helper ask in different ways if she can play with the toy. They gave seven answers that were all variants of "Ask again nicely." I let this process go on for a while in the hope that someone would suggest that she respect and listen to my answer and find something else to play with. Eventually, I pointed out that their solutions didn't seem to be working and that I was not going to say yes no matter how many times or how nicely the student asked me.

After this, a member of the audience suggested that she say, "Okay," and find a different toy. We practiced this solution. At the end of the lesson, as with other lessons, I searched for something catchy to help students remember what we talked about. This can be a joke someone made, a memorable quote, a song, a silly story, or an interactive chant.

During future class sessions, I followed up by asking students, "What do we do when we hear the word *no?*" or "Tell me about a time when someone said no to you this week. What did you do?" When students told stories in which they listened when someone told them no, the whole class acknowledged their good work with a round of applause.

This lesson is an example of one we teach with a concrete goal in mind. We want to teach students to respect and listen to the word *no.* While we could simply tell students this message in much less time than the previously described lesson, the question-based approach is more effective because it engages students in an exercise of discovery. They, not the adult, create the solution, and thus they are more likely to remember and act on the lesson learned. Once we have cocreated a word or concept, students' new language can be used to solve other problems as they emerge.

I Don't Want to Play with You

The year after I first taught the "No means no" lesson just described, we began to see an increase in relational aggression among the lower grades on the playground. Kindergartners and first graders began gaining power over others by saying, "I don't want to play with you." During guidance lessons and on the playground, we reminded students of the word *okay*, which we had taught previously. We helped students practice saying okay and playing with someone else when their peers tried to control them. After two weeks of review, students reported that the behavior pattern changed. Now, students who were trying to control others found themselves standing alone while targets enjoyed recess with one another. As a result, they chose to play with others without trying to control them.

Friends, Enemies, and Classmates

As a result of inaccurate, but common, thought processes, students often assign one of two labels to peers: *friends* or *enemies*. When young people assume that any peer who isn't their friend must be their enemy, they often choose to mistreat nonfriend peers. The following lesson addresses these issues by helping students see a third possibility.

I begin by drawing three columns on the board. In the left column, we brainstorm the ways in which friends interact with one another. In the right column, we brainstorm a list of how enemies interact. Then I ask students what other options exist. I often draw a parallel to the teaching staff at a school: Some teachers are close friends, and other teachers are neither friends nor enemies. I ask the class how the latter group of teachers interacts. We name this relationship as it relates to students and brainstorm possible interactions. Young people often call the people with whom they have this relationship classmates or schoolmates. Some students differentiate between people they are "friends with" and people they are "friendly to."

A fourth-grade class at the Bean school created the following lists of behaviors, describing three possible connections between people:

We can be friends. This means . . .

- We hang out together.

- We help each other.

- We play with each other.

- We stick up for each other.

- We like each other.

- We trust each other.

We can be classmates but not friends. This means . . .

- It's okay if we don't like each other.

- We are polite to each other.

- We are not mean to each other.

- We help each other with schoolwork and during emergencies.

- We may choose to stay away from each other.

- We may choose not to play with each other.

- We do not stop each other from having friends.

- We do not try to hurt each other.

We can be enemies. This means . . .

- We try to hurt each other's body and/or feelings.

- We make fun of each other.

- We stop each other from having friends.

- We start or spread rumors or lie about each other.

The Bean school does not allow enemies, and if we act like enemies we will have consequences.

Although most groups create similar lists, I have found it essential to re-create the contents of this list from scratch with each new class. It is the act of thinking about these categories and interactions that changes attitudes and perceptions. When students brainstorm the behaviors that fall into each category, they learn the lesson more deeply.

Over the past three years, Bean school staff have created many such lists, both in classrooms and during informal mediations between students. I now find that teachers and students at the Bean school spontaneously use the concept of classmates when discussing how young people could be interacting with a peer they are having trouble with. The idea of a third type of relationship, neither friend nor enemy, has become embedded in the school's culture, and both teachers and students use it often.

MODELING SOCIAL NORMS

Adults model social norms in many ways beyond conscious choice of language. We can model concern for all students, how to let small problems go, a work ethic, and resiliency. We can model the norms we hope to incorporate into school culture by being willing to own and share our own emotions in appropriate ways. For example, when I am sad or angry about something in my life, I sometimes choose to tell students, who might otherwise interpret my body language to indicate that I am angry with them. When it is appropriate to tell students how we feel, we model how to recognize, take ownership for, and deal with emotions. I often share feelings of pride, joy, and excitement with students, thus showing them they also have the right to be proud of their accomplishments. Of course, it is important to strike a balance between sharing with students and maintaining a professional distance. It is also important, as Bluestein (2003) emphasizes in her article about I-messages, to avoid making students feel responsible for our emotions. When it is appropriate to share our emotions with students, it can be a powerful tool to help them understand and handle their own emotions in productive ways.

In everyday interactions with students, staff can also encourage honesty as a core value. When young people are willing to tell the truth about their antisocial behavior, they become able to meet their needs effectively. Students need to know that they can tell the truth about what they did wrong without experiencing anger or rejection from adults they care about. Thus we encourage honesty when we maintain positive feeling tone throughout the discipline process and make it clear to students that we will like them no matter what they do. We can make it more likely that students will continue to tell the truth when we praise them by saying, "Thank you for telling the truth. I know that's not always easy." In saying this, we recognize how difficult it is for adults and young people alike to admit mistakes to people we care about. In addition, when we adults openly admit and learn from our own mistakes, we model the traits we hope to instill in students.

Customs, Practices, and the School Environment

Even minor school customs and practices impact school culture. The subtle physical characteristics, customs, and practices of a school may be inconsistent with the messages of a bullying prevention program. The physical school environment— namely, buildings upkeep and the signs, decorations, and messages posted on the walls—affects school atmosphere. School customs and traditions communicate school values. These traditions include which behaviors and traits are recognized at awards assemblies and how schools communicate respect for diverse student backgrounds.

It may be difficult for staff to recognize the physical and emotional climate of their own school because of their daily immersion in that environment. It is also helpful to remember that those in the majority often fail to understand how seemingly minor practices impact individuals belonging to minority groups. Assessing school climate can be as easy as asking a diverse group of trusted outsiders or parents of new students to visit; walk the halls; sit in on classes; and tell us what they see, hear, and feel. Surveys and discussions with staff, students, and community members can help us understand the messages we send through school traditions. To remedy unfriendly practices, school staff may choose to expand student recognition beyond the honor roll in order to recognize students for a wider variety of accomplishments. Staff may reexamine the school mascot or team name to ensure that it implies respect and inclusion. Schools may provide free yearbooks and entrance to school events in order to include economically disadvantaged youth. Lyn Mikel Brown's best practices statement, "Creating Safe, Fair, and Responsive Schools," provides valuable insight in relation to this topic. She writes:

> [Safe, fair, and responsive schools] examine (through self-study) school practices that unwittingly support unfairness, competition, and divisiveness among students, such as the uneven distribution of resources, and eliminate or alter practices that privilege some students more than others. (n.d., para. 11)

The following example shows how a minor shift in school practices can help focus attention on fairness and inclusion. In fall 2006, we were about to elect our student council members at the Bean school. I attended a staff workshop in Michigan, where I met a student council advisor who holds blind elections. In her school, young people vote on statements of the candidates' goals for the school without knowing which student wrote which statement. When I came back to the Bean school after the workshop and suggested this alternative method of selecting student council members to our teachers, they were enthusiastic. After the elections were over, I asked students why they thought we had changed the process and what they thought of the change. They told me that the new process allowed less popular or new students with good ideas to be elected. Several students said they preferred this new way of conducting elections because they didn't have to worry about how their friends would feel if they didn't vote for them. We talked about this election process as an example of schoolwide inclusion. When students who were not elected to the student council asked to be involved, we supplemented our six-member student council with a 20-member school service corps. These two groups now work together to run community food drives and raise money to provide chickens and goats for hungry families in the third world (through the Heifer project; www.heifer.org) and to purchase new playground equipment and design school T-shirts.

CORRECTING MISPERCEPTIONS ABOUT SOCIAL NORMS

In addition to looking critically at common practices, we can help students correct misperceptions about social norms. Social norms interventions are common and successful tools to change undesired behaviors. The effectiveness of student-based social norms interventions stems from the natural human need to be in the middle of the normal curve. Jeffrey writes, "Social norms research shows that peer influences are based more on the perceived rather than the actual peer norm. When perceived peer influences are corrected, individuals are more likely to express healthy beliefs and attitudes" (2004, p. 8). The first step, then, is to help students understand that most of their peers share their positive values. Jeffrey writes:

> Bully victimization rates average between 7% and 15%. The majority of students do not get bullied. The great majority of students are not bullies. A social norms campaign to decrease bullying would inform a school community that bullying was not a normative event in their community, most students do not report being bullied, and most students value cooperation and respect. Moreover, the campaign would endorse the idea that the average student in the community believes that students should be supported to speak up for each other's welfare. A social norms campaign is not a denial of a problem, but rather is an assertion of the actual prosocial values of the majority, i.e., the actual social norm. The key messages might include that members of the school community do not need to feel alone, that protecting each other is a valued act, and that courage in the face of injustice is a major community value. (p. 8)

When I talk with young people about bullying, I often hear misperceptions about normative values and behavior. Those who are bullied often tell me, "Everyone picks on me." Through talking with numerous young people, I find that both youth who bully and those who are bullied commonly misperceive their school environment and see the majority of peers as in support of the bully.

The illustration on the next page captures a common view of the social environment in schools. Yet when I talk with teachers and observe in classrooms and on the playground, I consistently see only a small number of active bullies. Most students are empathetic, concerned about others' feelings, and reluctant to tease or bully. Thus bullies' and targets' perceptions seem to differ dramatically from reality. Why do they believe that everyone in the school sides with young people who bully?

To help young people answer this question, I often begin my student workshops with the following exercise. Before the workshop, I instruct two student actors to sit near the front of the audience and, on cue, for one to begin teasing the other. I rebuke the student who bullies, but when I turn away the teasing continues. In nearly all of the more than 500 workshops I have led, the audience begins by silently watching the teasing. They often laugh in apparent embarrassment. After a short time, I ask the student actors what they observed from their classmates during the bullying scenario. They answer that their peers watched silently and laughed. I ask if this happens in real bullying situations, and they reply that it does. My next questions are "What do silence and laughter tell the bully?" and "What messages do silence and laughter send to the target?" Young people of all ages tell me that targets and bullies interpret silence and laughter as an indication that their peers support and agree with youth who bully.

When young people who bully believe that peers support their behavior, they may feel powerful and in control, which makes them more likely to continue their hurtful behavior. When young people who are bullied believe that their peers support the students who bully them, they may interpret this as an indication that they deserve to be treated poorly. Research on bystander attitudes shows that many bystanders are quietly sympathetic toward targets of bullying. Atlas and Pepler (1998) found that 80 to 90 percent of children reported that they found

What Targets and Bullies See

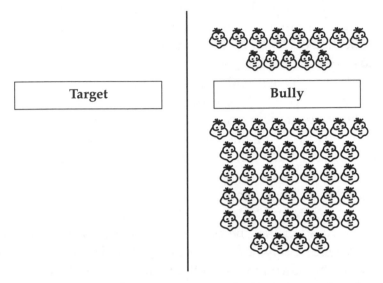

it unpleasant to watch bullying, yet only 11 percent of students reported that they intervened directly to stop bullying. In Australia, Rigby and Slee (1991) found that the majority of students were opposed to bullying and felt sympathetic toward victims. Salmivalli and Voeten (2004) wrote:

> The majority of school-aged children and adolescents have attitudes that are clearly opposed to bulling, i.e., they think it is a wrong thing to do . . . and most students have intentions to help or support the victim rather than to join in. . . . Anti-bullying attitudes clearly outweigh pro-bullying attitudes in all age groups studied, i.e., students generally seem to consider bullying as inappropriate rather than acceptable. . . . An interesting paradox arises: most students believe that bullying is wrong, and they think that one should try to help the victims. Nevertheless, most students do not express their disapproval to peers who bully, and actually do nothing to intervene or support the victim. . . . As research on participant roles . . . has shown, it is common to join in bullying, or encourage the bully by laughing or gathering around to "see the show." (p. 247)

Leading to the same conclusion are results of the Olweus Bully-Victim Questionnaire (BVQ; Olweus, 1996), an anonymous student survey that examines bullying behaviors, staff actions, and bystander attitudes and behavior. I have used the BVQ and other questionnaires to survey students in elementary and middle schools in New England and have talked with others who have used the BVQ across the United States. The results of these surveys consistently show that only a small minority of students believe that targets deserve to be bullied. Yet students who object to bullying report that they often watch silently when bullying occurs. After talking with young people and reviewing the research, I believe thediagram on the next page represents a more accurate picture of a class or school. This diagram is an adaptation of the Olweus bullying circle (Olweus, Limber, & Mihalic, 1997).

The question, then, becomes why so many caring bystanders silently watch bullying. When we begin listening to bystanders, in person and through the brilliant interviews in the video *Let's Get Real* (Chasnoff, 2004), several reasons become immediately clear. Bystanders are afraid of becoming targets of bullying themselves, see direct confrontation as the best intervention, and believe they are the only ones who object to bullying.

As discussed in chapters 1 and 2, schoolwide bullying prevention programs should incorporate interventions to protect witnesses who report bullying. With adults taking an active role to ensure bystander safety, we can remedy the first reason students remain silent. Also discussed in chapter 1 are the shortcomings of an emphasis on direct confrontation, which is clearly neither safe nor effective in most situations. Through the skills-based interventions described in chapter 3, we can help students develop a wide range of effective solutions. In the ensuing paragraphs, I will discuss interventions to tackle the last of the three reasons bystanders remain silent: their belief that they are alone in objecting to bullying.

Correcting misperceived social norms involves presenting inarguable data clearly showing that many students share positive beliefs and attitudes. Social norms interventions have been successfully implemented to reduce smoking and high-risk drinking in high schools and colleges (Kluger, 2001). Hanson writes:

What Targets and Bullies See

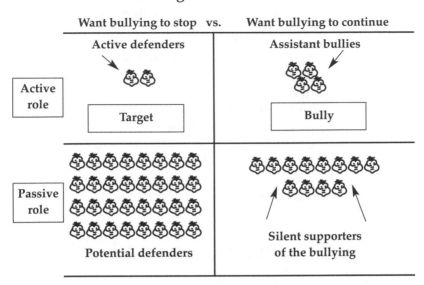

"The study clearly demonstrates that students' perceptions of the drinking norms on their campus is by far the strongest predictor of the amount of alcohol personally consumed," said Michael Haines, Director of the National Social Norms Resource Center. "Furthermore, colleges whose prevention efforts reduce students' misperceptions of peer drinking reduce high-risk drinking and negative consequences. That is what social norms campaigns are designed to do." (n.d., para. 2)

Similarly, my experience sharing specific survey data relating to attitudes toward bullying with elementary school students has been quite successful, especially when the data come from students' own schools. School staff can conduct a simple but influential survey by asking students "When you see bullying, do you usually think the target deserves the bullying?" The vast majority of students predictably report that students who are bullied do not deserve the bullying. I have found it effective to compile student answers to this one question in a pie chart, thus clearly showing the percentages of students who believe and don't believe targets deserve bullying. When I show students this data, they often express relief and become more animated during further discussions.

As with any intervention, we must follow up with students beyond the first presentation of data. Teicher writes:

> The starting point is to present kids with credible bullying data from their own school, not a state or national average. The professors developed a survey for schools, funded by the New Jersey and US Departments of Education (http://socialnormsurveys.hws.edu). Once they gather data, educators need to send consistent messages about the true norms throughout the year. "You can't just hang a few posters," Perkins says. Some schools, for instance, incorporate the information into their orientations and curriculum and post statistics on screensavers in computer labs. (2006, para. 6–7)

REPLACING DYSFUNCTIONAL SOCIAL NORMS

While it is clear that many students and staff share positive social norms, such as empathy and caring, schools also perpetuate dysfunctional social norms, which can be detrimental to a bullying prevention program. Staff and students can combat these destructive norms by recognizing their effects and striving to replace them with more positive norms. In the following paragraphs, I will discuss in detail two common dysfunctional social norms and effective interventions to replace them with more useful norms.

Tattling

One of the most frequent questions I receive from educators who attend my bullying prevention trainings is "What should I do about tattling?" Understandably, teachers find it problematic when students interrupt their academic lessons to tell them about other students' minor offenses. Many techniques for discouraging tattling exist in common usage and children's books. One recent children's book describes a scenario in which a student comes to the teacher reporting that another student called someone in the class mean names. The teacher replies, "We don't try to fix problems that don't belong to us. . . . Your job is to take care of you" (Ranson, 2005, p. 13). I would prefer to teach students a different lesson—namely, to help their peers when they are in trouble or experience bullying. The lesson we choose, whether it be to speak up or remain silent, has far-reaching consequences for schools and communities.

The problem remains that, even when I say to students, "If anyone is being hurt or needs help, I want to know. If not, maybe I don't need to know," I still encounter students who report that a peer "cut" them in line, is using the wrong colored pencil, or is on the field without her boots on. The question, then, is how to listen to and value students' concerns while still being able to teach. My discovery of an alternative intervention was driven by three major realizations.

My first realization came from working with middle and high school staff. They told me of their struggles with a strong code of silence among students. Teens are often reluctant to tell adults about what they see in the halls, what goes on in the locker rooms, and what happens in the back of the classroom. The word *tattletale* is used in a derogatory fashion. Many students learn from their elementary school teachers that adults don't want to hear about aggression directed at peers. Aggressive peers take advantage of this message to reinforce the idea that it isn't cool to tell adults and get others in trouble. Television, teen books, adults, and young people use words like *rat, fink,* and *squealer.* Thorne writes:

> There is a stereotypical association of younger kids and of girls of all ages with complaining to adults about the behavior of other kids. The word "tattling" is often used for this behavior, which conveys the telling of tales, secrets, and thus the betrayal of one's kind. The negative connotation builds in a judgment I want to query. Sometimes the less powerful, or those not trained to be physically aggressive, have little recourse except to complain to adults. (1993, p. 77)

My second realization came after I asked myself why students tattle. After observing students in the classroom and at recess year after year, I came to the conclusion that the primary motivations for tattling are to get the teacher's attention or to control teachers or peers. In either situation, many educators unknowingly provide tattling students with the attention or control they seek. This attention may take the form of exasperation or anger, but it still reinforces tattling behavior, therefore making it more likely that students will tattle again. For children seeking power, the power to exasperate the teacher can be very attractive. Even if the attention comes in the form of a calm, brief, in-the-moment lesson about the difference between tattling and telling, the student has still earned the teacher's full attention.

My third realization came from looking at parallels between schools and other social institutions. Teachers, physicians, and police officers are all busy and overworked. For all three groups, maintaining the safety of the people with whom they work is a primary responsibility. Suppose physicians began discouraging patients from calling with less urgent health concerns. Suppose a police department began telling citizens to deal with less serious problems on their own. Suppose witnesses calling 911 were told that they shouldn't have called because they shouldn't be concerned about crimes that don't affect them directly. It seems clear that if these changes were to occur, we would live in a far more dangerous world.

The tattling intervention that emerged from these three realizations combines ongoing skills teaching with a specific response in the moment when children tattle. First and foremost, as school staff we should make it clear to students that we want to hear their concerns. Without this core understanding, we undermine our work to create bullying prevention programs based on the principles of Neighborhood Watch, described in chapter 1. At the Bean school, we tell students at the beginning of the year that we want to hear about their problems and concerns. We discourage students from interrupting instruction and enforce a system of consequences for interrupting, except in emergencies. We tell them that some behaviors are against school rules and some are not and that it is our job to decide when to intervene. We explain that if they tell us about something we choose not to deal with directly, we may suggest a possible solution, or we may just thank them for telling us and move on. After making our plan clear, we follow through. We listen to what students tell us, thank them for telling us about their concerns, and decide whether or not to act. When students bring us small problems, we quickly give them advice or thank them and move on in order not to reinforce their behavior.

When we combine this specific in-the-moment strategy with ongoing lessons to help students develop, implement, and refine social problem solving skills, we help students differentiate between big and small problems and use several solutions to attempt to solve small problems before approaching adults. This combination intervention of removing reinforcement for tattling and teaching problem-solving skills worked to reduce levels of tattling at the Bean school. Our work shows that it is possible for school staff to break down the code of silence while also maintaining consistent standards in order to teach without interruption.

Forced Apologies

A second common and dysfunctional social norm is the practice of forcing apologies from aggressive youth. I have found forced apologies to be an ineffective means of teaching young people to care about the impact of their behavior on others. Apologies made under duress are unlikely to be genuine, can help aggressive youth feel better without changing their behavior, and pressure targets of aggression to forgive before they are ready to do so.

When adults tell young people to apologize, we teach them to lie. When students apologize immediately and see their apology accepted, they may feel less remorse about their behavior. They learn that words can undo actions, and they become more likely to continue acting aggressively toward their peers because they know they can erase their harm by saying they're sorry. Thus forced apologies can act to reduce remorse in aggressive youth and reinforce aggression as an acceptable solution to social problems.

Targets of aggressive behavior are pressured by immediate and forced apologies to forgive aggressors, even when they know aggressors don't really feel sorry for their behavior.

Encouraging targets to say, "It's okay" or "I forgive you," teaches them to lie because it is unlikely that targets really think it's okay or are ready to forgive. Forgiveness is an intensely personal decision, and we should be careful not to put social pressure on young people to forgive when they still feel angry, hurt, or scared. It is not the responsibility of targets to help aggressors feel better about their behavior.

Genuine apologies can be emotionally moving for both parties and have great value. However, they must be freely chosen as the result of independent thought. Compelled apologies cheapen the statement "I'm sorry," reducing it to a formula of polite social obligation rather than representing a heartfelt statement of remorse. True apologies must communicate an effort to change future behavior to avoid hurting others again.

Teaching young people to care about the impact of their behavior on others is essential to our work as parents and educators. Instead of forcing apologies, we can help aggressive youth learn from their behavior when we encourage them to acknowledge their actions, hold them fully accountable for their behavior, use small and consistent consequences for aggressive behavior, maintain positive relationships with students whether they behave or misbehave, and model full responsibility for one's actions.

While true apologies cannot be compelled, acknowledgment can. We can lead students to acknowledge their actions by telling them to make written or verbal statements such as "I knocked you down" or "I broke your toy." We can help students develop empathy by asking them to mentally revisit the incident, remember what the target said and did, and think about what this tells them about how the target felt. As students develop empathy, we can prompt them to add a second statement to their acknowledgment about the effect of their behavior, such as "I know that hurt" or "I know that toy was important to you." I have found written statements to be more effective than verbal statements because verbal acknowledgments often transform into unfelt apologies out of habit, whereas staff can screen written acknowledgments for apologies, criticism of the target, and excuses. Acknowledgment places the responsibility for change on the aggressor, builds honesty, and does not create a social obligation for the target to show forgiveness. Thus, while compelled apology often makes aggressors feel better, compelled acknowledgment often makes targets feel better while also helping aggressors build conscience.

HOLDING YOUNG PEOPLE ACCOUNTABLE

Holding young people fully accountable for their behavior rests on one assumption: All behavior is the result of a choice between options. When our thinking and language shift to reflect the idea that all behavior is primarily the result of a choice, young people are more likely to take responsibility for their actions. We help young people best when we hold them accountable, regardless of their intent. Many young people seem to believe that by stating that they intended no harm, they can avoid responsibility for their actions. The truth in most situations is that harm is done and is the result of a choice. When adults accept the statement "It was an accident" at face value, young people can learn to avoid responsibility by claiming everything they do is accidental. We can acknowledge that they meant no harm, but we must also hold students responsible for the impact of their actions on others and communicate that it is their job to change their hurtful behavior in the future.

When we enforce small and consistent consequences for hurtful behavior, we teach young people to be kind to others. Consequences are an important element in learning responsibility. When young people see that their behavior has a negative impact on themselves, they are more likely to consider the possibility that their behavior may also have a negative impact on others. Predictable, small, and consistent consequences delivered with positive feeling tone teach cause-and-effect thinking and self-control. Consequences should be based on specific behaviors, and staff should not alter consequences for "good kids" or when children apologize or claim that they didn't mean it. We do not help young people mature when we back down or give in.

Young people are more likely to attempt change when they feel safe. It isn't easy to develop new habits, and children need support. Aggressive youth need positive relationships with adults who do not show anger toward them when they misbehave. To this end, adults can monitor the tone of their interactions with students. I often tell young people, "No matter what you did, I still care about you." Adult behavior is also a powerful determining factor for student change. When we take responsibility for our own unkind words, tell the truth, and work to change and improve, we show students how to do the same.

INDIRECT HARASSMENT

Another trend driven by social norms and school culture is the presence or absence of indirect harassment, taking the form of offhand jokes and comments and often not meant to cause damage to another person. Students frequently fail to understand the impact of indirect harassment. Staff and students alike often don't notice when someone calls a movie gay or says that someone throws like a girl, yet these comments send strong messages reinforcing unfair value systems and uneven power dynamics. Using *gay* as a synonym for bad or stupid sends a message that being homosexual is bad and can make gay, lesbian, bisexual, transgender, and questioning (GBLTQ) youth feel less safe. Saying that someone throws like a girl implies that females are inferior in physical endeavors. This powerful message about the ability and athleticism of girls and women can be internalized.

Frequent indirect harassment can lead to more serious harassment and violence as individuals begin to see prejudice as normative. Bigoted youth hear their peers' statements and are more likely to threaten, harass, or attack because they believe their biases are supported by the majority.

Indirect harassment is common in schools, and students and educators tell me that derogatory language related to gender and sexual orientation is the most frequent type of indirect harassment they witness. These observations are confirmed by a Harris Interactive survey of 3,450 students and 1,011 teachers across the United States ("From Teasing to Torment," 2005). The following table summarizes some of the findings of this survey.

Harris Interactive survey questions	Percentage of teens who answered "very often" or "often"
At your school, how often do you hear students making the following types of remarks?	
1. Homophobic remarks	52
2. Racist remarks	26
3. Sexist remarks	51
4. Negative religious remarks	10
5. At your school, how often do you hear students use the expression,"That's so gay" or "You're so gay"?	69

The California Safe Schools Coalition completed a parallel analysis of harassment based on sexual orientation and gender nonconformity. Their key findings are summarized as follows:

Finding 1: Harassment based on actual or perceived sexual orientation is pervasive. . . .

Finding 2: Students who are harassed based on actual or perceived sexual orientation report weaker connections to school, adults, and community. . . .

Finding 3: Students who are harassed based on actual or perceived sexual orientation reported higher levels of risk on a wide array of academic, health, and safety measures. (Russell et al., 2006, p. 1)

I have developed a five-step process, which may help you develop your own approach, to discuss with young people the common usage of the word *gay* as a negative adjective. First, I tell students that I know when they use *gay* as an adjective they don't mean harm. This puts many young people at ease. Second, I cite the common statistic that 10 percent of the population is gay or lesbian. I point out that many people question their sexual orientation. Third, I tell students that those who identify themselves as gay or lesbian or are questioning their sexual orientation feel less safe when they hear *gay* used in a derogatory fashion. Next, I acknowledge that in the audience there are individuals with widely ranging beliefs. Whether they believe it is right or wrong to be gay or lesbian isn't the point. The point is that every school has a few bigots who believe they have the right to hurt others who are gay or lesbian. When these bigots hear many people using the word *gay* in a derogatory fashion, they feel justified and empowered to use aggression. Young people can begin to understand the effects of indirect harassment through discussion, hearing from others who have experienced discrimination, and imagining what it must feel like to be discriminated against. We can proceed to discuss with young people how they can react when they hear indirect harassment. Although it is not the case in other bullying scenarios, telling the aggressor to stop often does work well in these situations. Some good techniques to use when speaking up directly include a personal statement (e.g., "I have a gay friend, and that kind of language hurts him"), a direct request (e.g., "Please stop talking like that"), and a contradiction of the stereotype (e.g., "If he throws like a girl, then he must be pretty good"). We should also discuss alternative solutions for students who do not feel comfortable speaking up directly against indirect harassment. Primary solutions include changing the subject, leaving conversations in which this language is being used, and telling adults.

Staff-based disciplinary interventions can be as simple as Saufler's "ten-second intervention." He writes:

> This intervention is designed to address inappropriate language that is not directed at any one person with the intention of hurting. It's more for the type of language that adults have come to believe is OK because "[students] all talk that way." Like when one friend says to another, "That shirt is so gay." All it involves is the teacher turning to whoever said the inappropriate statement and saying something like, "That's inappropriate language for school; please don't say it again,"

and then moving on—no lecture, argument, or further discussion. (2006, para. 3)

Saufler points out that if 30 teachers in a school each used this intervention six times a day, for a total of one minute per teacher, students schoolwide would hear positive statements about community values 180 times a day.

GENDER-BASED CONCERNS

In addition to addressing indirect harassment, we can and should also address issues of gender. Gender-based stereotypes, prejudice, and discrimination are important topics of discussion for students of all ages because much bullying in the preteen and teen years is based on the enforcement of narrow gender roles among both boys and girls. Lyn Mikel Brown, author of the essential book *Girlfighting: Betrayal and Rejection Among Girls*, writes:

> Unfortunately, girls often gain power by using the tools of sexism on each other in ways that maintain the broader patriarchal landscape, such as using the language of sexual objectification—calling other girls hos, sluts, and bitches—or judging other girls and women against narrow images of beauty. Interrupting girlfighting means advocating for gender diversity—for many ways to be girls of substance—and offering girls opportunities to try on different identities, to experience more visible avenues to power, to challenge sexist, racist, homophobic arrangements, to feel in control and to create environments that feel good to them. This won't get rid of all girlfighting and shouldn't—girls should be encouraged to feel angry and fight in constructive ways about the things that really matter to them. But I believe it will work to reduce the misogynistic forms of girlfighting that so prevail in our culture. (2005, p. 203)

Similarly, Kimmel and Mahler (2003) found that bullying among preteen and teenage boys often rests on an unrealistic and narrow view of masculinity. They point to the destructive effects of common adolescent name-calling based on sexual orientation and aimed at marginalizing young men who are not perceived as truly masculine. When we address and broaden definitions of both femininity and masculinity, we help young people discard prejudice and the fear of not fitting into stereotypes. Brown (n.d.) proposes a useful list of best practices to go about addressing these issues with both boys and girls in upper elementary school, middle school, and high school. The following discussion focuses on techniques to address narrow gender expectations in elementary school.

⚜

We can and should begin addressing gender stereotypes with adult-based interventions to prohibit harassment and gender discrimination. Next, we can focus students' attention on the underlying assumptions they learn. At very young ages, children enforce rigid and narrow gender expectations on themselves and one another. Kindergartners and first graders tell their peers what girls and boys are supposed to do or not do. For example, a fourth grader told me in a 2006 class discussion, "My brother is in first grade. He loves to dance, but he doesn't tell his friends because he's afraid of being teased." Books, television, and movies teach narrow stereotypes and model rejection of young people who stray outside of stereotypes. At every grade level, we can counteract culture by helping young people broaden their views of the traits and interests of girls and boys.

One of the primary techniques to broaden gender stereotypes concerns being role models. As they are in society as a whole, gender stereotypes are prevalent and accepted in many educational circles. Just as it is important for staff to challenge assumptions about race in schools, we should refute statements and assumptions that perpetuate gender stereotypes. One example of the continued presence of gender stereotyping comes from a staff training institute on childhood psychopathology for educators and counselors I attended in 2006. Two of five highly regarded speakers made statements stereotyping males and females. One said that he rewards boys with sports-related toys and girls with dolls. Another presenter stated that women use shopping for stress relief. She asked rhetorically what men do for this purpose and answered her own question by pretending to use a TV remote to flip between channels. The audience of undergraduates and mental health professionals laughed comfortably.

School staff members often support stereotypes that limit both boys and girls by making "humorous" comments reinforcing gender stereotypes in the teachers' room, during staff meetings, and in other informal settings. These stereotypes are so omnipresent, they are often invisible. With attention and effort, though, we can challenge assumptions. When we hear a colleague saying that a male student is a "typical boy," we can ask if all boys are active or if all boys hate reading. When we hear a colleague saying that a girl who spreads rumors is "just being a mean third-grade girl," we can talk about boys or girls who do not fit the pattern.

Educators often ask me about research showing clear differences between boys and girls. While this research often presents differences as fundamental and unchangeable, I believe that they are largely culturally constructed and changeable. Even when we observe patterns of gender differences, it is clear that not all individuals fit into stereotypical gender roles. When we emphasize inherent differences between males and females, we run the risk of lowering our standards for girls or boys in certain areas because we assume that they possess different abilities.

We can address gender issues with students directly when we connect historical events to current cultural expectations. Students and adults are often unaware of historical injustice based on gender, race, religion, and other categories. Their strong idealistic reaction to learning about overt discrimination often provides the interest and motivation for them to focus critically on the present. For example, young people are often astonished to find out that women were not allowed to vote in the United States until 1920. When we teach students about women's lengthy struggle to gain the vote throughout the world, we can explore issues of power and the ways in which gender roles limit individuals and groups. We can then draw the parallel to what games and hobbies boys and girls are encouraged and discouraged from pursuing in the present. We can point out the roles our students play in reinforcing gender stereotypes and use their outrage about historical discrimination to break down the gender discrimination they participate in every day. We can draw similar parallels between discussions of slavery and segregation and exclusion of marginalized youth in the school environment.

In addition to historical parallels, discussing literature also provides opportunities to address the restrictions that gender roles put on characters and our students. In many books written for children or teens, we can find examples of gender stereotyping, rigid role definitions, and fear or anger in response to characters that do not fit narrow gender expectations. We can use literature to spark fascinating conversations about how we limit individuals when we say art is an activity for girls, race cars are for boys, girls do housework, and boys do yard chores. It is often easier for elementary school students to begin discussing gender issues in the imaginary context of literature than it is for them to immediately discuss their own lives.

One of many examples of this use of literature is my experience reading *Bridge to Terabithia* (Paterson, 1978) to a fourth-grade class at the Bean school in 2006. A similar analysis and use of discussion questions could be used with many other books. In the first chapter, we learned that the main character is a boy who loves to draw but hides his love because his father thinks art is for girls. When I asked students what they thought about this, I found both boys and girls outraged to think that someone should have to hide or give up a beloved hobby or interest. One girl in a recent discussion added, "It's especially hard to try to hide something from your parents," acknowledging the difficulty of pretending to be someone you are not around the people who love you. As the story continued, we noticed other examples of ways the main character and his sisters were treated differently.

After informally discussing gender limitations, we can use a variant of a well-known instructional exercise during which we draw two boxes on the board and label one *girls* and the other *boys*. While reading *Bridge to Terabithia*, I instructed students to listen for evidence of gender stereotypes and identify the interests, characteristics, hobbies, and other descriptors attributed to girls and boys. During the discussion, some students were outraged when certain characteristics were placed in one box or the other. Some students objected when they realized that in the culture of the 1970s, shopping, art, and hugs fit in the girls' box, while sports and playing in the mud fit in the boys' box. As we constructed boxes of masculinity and femininity based on evidence found in the book, students began to see gender divisions as limiting, unrealistic, and unnecessary. One student suggested we find a way to erase both boxes and make a third one called *people*.

After discussing gender roles in the world of books, we can encourage students to look critically at the present school environment and examine the expectations placed on boys and girls. By questioning gender roles, students become able to talk, without criticism, about girls who like to ride four-wheelers and boys who like to shop. They are in a position, based on our discussions of stereotypes and diversity, to contrast stereotypes with reality and to attach value to reality.

The exercise just described provides a painless introduction to basic concepts about gender roles. It helps teach young people that stereotypes exist, are communicated to individuals from many sources, and limit both boys and girls. The exercise also teaches young people to recognize and question the messages implicit in books, magazines, television, and movies.

Discussions of gender stereotypes naturally lead to discussions of what happens when individuals stray outside of culturally constructed boxes of acceptable behavior. When discussing this issue, we should address the following key questions:

- How do individuals and the media keep young people in narrowly defined boxes?

- What do peers do when they see young people acting in ways that defy these expectations?

- How can peers change those actions to allow each other to be who they really are?

In addition to the previously discussed interventions to combat narrow gender stereotypes, most important is our willingness to challenge peer gender stereotyping in the moment. When we hear boys saying, "Girls can't play soccer well" or hear girls chanting, "Girls go to college to get more knowledge; boys go to Jupiter to get more stupider," we can identify and question their underlying assumptions. For example, when a student told me at lunch recently, "Girls can't beat boys at tennis," I asked him if that meant that he could beat every single girl and woman alive at tennis. He thought for a moment and conceded that there were girls and women who could beat him. As adults, we are presented with many opportunities to help students move from oversimplified assumptions about individuals to more realistic and less limiting worldviews.

SUPPORTING INCLUSION

Establishing inclusion as a valued and supported social norm can help all students feel safe and valued. As I mentioned previously, exclusion is one of the most hurtful forms of bullying. Since students often exclude others in order to fit in and be popular, school culture interventions can be especially effective when they deemphasize popularity and make inclusion the accepted and expected default behavior.

Friendship Teams

I wrote in *Schools Where Everyone Belongs* about friendship teams, which involves recruiting empathetic and well-liked students to spend time with isolated youth. Creating and coaching teams of self-selected defenders can make schools safer and more inclusive for targets of bullying and all marginalized youth. In elementary schools, these teams can take several different forms. The first type of friendship team is created when an isolated student approaches a school staff member to ask for help making friends. Staff then recruit and train peers chosen by that student to invite the excluded student into group activities, tell others about the student's positive traits, and give the student supportive feedback about behavior that makes it hard for others to be friends with him. I meet with the isolated student and his friendship team weekly at lunchtime to review what they have done to help and what positive effects their behavior is having. These teams are usually short term and end when the isolated student seems to have made his own friends.

I initiate the second type of friendship team when the excluded student doesn't want to be involved, but I become aware that her peers are treating her as a scapegoat or excluding her. In this situation, I enlist other students to support the excluded student by learning positive ways to interact with her. I meet with these friendship teams weekly to practice strategies to ignore minor annoyances and give positive feedback for prosocial behaviors. Although the isolated student is not in the room, I do not allow discussion of her behavior behind the student's back. The focus is solely on planning and implementing helping acts by the team members. These bystanders move from participating in or ignoring bullying to supporting the target, thus encouraging peers to do the same. Usually, the excluded student knows about the friendship team, but sometimes I don't involve the student at all.

The third option for friendship teams, which I have found effective for fifth grade and up, is to create teams not focused on helping any particular excluded student. These teams instead focus on identifying and including isolated youth schoolwide. As with all types of friendship teams, it is important to meet on a regular basis to review what the team has done and help them see their own effectiveness. Without ongoing support and the belief that they can enact change, students are likely to stop reaching out to include peers.

For all types of friendship teams, it is important that our volunteers approach isolated peers out of a wish to get to know them better, rather than out of pity. They should be thinking, "If I get to know someone new, I might make a really cool friend." Adults can encourage this attitude through the language we use to recruit and mentor friendship teams.

Advisory Panels and School Watch Teams

At the elementary level, we can also create a group of self-selected students to serve as an advisory panel for the school's bullying prevention program. We can ask this advisory panel for advice when we see a pattern of antisocial behavior and encourage them to be honest witnesses when they observe aggression.

At the middle school and high school levels, we can recruit a more formal team, modeled after Neighborhood Watch programs. Recruiting for such a group involves talking with the student body as a whole about bullying and the impact bystanders can have on school climate and then inviting students to join the team. In order to make sure students truly want to make a difference as bystanders, we should require several independent steps to join the School Watch team. These steps may include going to the guidance office to get an application, completing and turning in a bullying observation diary, and attending an informational session after school or during recess. The process of keeping a bullying observation diary not only ensures the dedication of students but also raises their consciousness, alerts staff to the reality of bullying in the school environment, increases students' motivation to make a difference, and provides real-life scenarios for practice sessions. Following are the instructions I give to students for completing bullying observation diaries.

Directions for Keeping a Bullying Observation Diary

Please help us make your school a safer place by using this diary to record your observations of the following three types of behavior:

1. Indirect bullying and harassment. These casual comments are often made in a joking manner and are not directed at

any one person in particular. These comments make fun of or criticize women, men, people whose appearance or abilities are different, people of a particular background or race, or people who are gay or lesbian. The following are a few examples I have heard in schools: "That test was so gay" (implying that being gay is bad), "She jewed me down" (implying that Jews are cheap), and "He throws like a girl" (implying that girls don't throw well).

2. Direct bullying and harassment. Some examples of these behaviors are name-calling, insulting, making gestures, and any other behaviors that make others feel bad.

3. Threats and hitting. This category includes any form of physical contact meant to hurt, such as kicking, slapping, pushing, or other unwanted touching.

As soon as possible after each of four incidents, please record the location of the incident and the answers to the following two questions. Please do not record the real names of the individuals involved.

1. What did the bully or bullies do or say? Be specific and record as many details as possible.

2. What did the people observing the incident do or say? Were they silent? Did they laugh? Did they join the bullying? Did they say or do something to stop the behavior? Be specific and record details.

Once a School Watch team is formed, staff should train and support members to help them develop skills and use those skills to improve school culture. As with friendship teams, the effectiveness of these groups relies on ongoing skill practice, support, and feedback showing students their positive impact.

Peer Tutoring and Advisor-Advisee Programs

Besides friendship teams, advisory panels, and School Watch teams, school staff can help connect high-status and low-status peers through peer-tutoring programs and advisor-advisee programs. Fuchs, Fuchs, Mathes, and Martinez (2002) found that peer tutoring raises the status of tutored students. Aronson argues that engaging students as partners in reaching important common goals can build bonds between individuals from different groups. He writes:

> Hostility between groups can form and become entrenched very easily. . . . If schools want to decrease the animosity among cliques, repressing it is not enough. Schools have to offer students a [meaningful] common goal that they can all work toward together, within a structure that supports a positive sense of belonging. (2000, p. 119)

SUMMARY AND CONCLUSIONS

Students and staff constantly transmit school culture to each other. Older students show and tell younger students how to behave, and new students learn quickly. Students' and adults' understanding of which behaviors are normal and valued drives everyday interactions and responses to conflict. When we do not address dysfunctional social norms that govern staff and student behavior, peer culture can negate our efforts to prevent bullying. When we identify, question, and work to change language, norms, and culture through teaching and discussion, we can have a deep and long-lasting impact on school climate. Implementing interventions that clarify and reshape social norms gives students an active voice and enlists them as partners in bullying prevention.

Chapter 6

Student-Created Videos and Peace Day Assemblies

This chapter focuses on two specific culture- and norm-based interventions that have had striking effects on peer culture and bystander behavior at the Bean school: student-created videos and Peace Day assemblies. These interventions are effective because they shift ownership of changing school culture from staff to students. By doing this, we affirm the power students have to question and consciously change common beliefs, attitudes, and behavior.

STUDENT-CREATED VIDEOS

I have found student-created videos to be a profound and effective teaching tool for building positive peer culture. My family got our first television set when I was 12 years old. Given that I grew up in a pre-television culture of oral story-telling, my native language for self-expression is the spoken word. Most of our students, however, have spent their entire lives inundated with video images, and electronic media have become their primary means of receiving information. Student-created videos allow students to move from passively watching to actively creating and sharing. Video production is also exciting for young people because it allows them to become proficient in technology and skills many of the adults in their lives have not mastered. When adults learn new skills alongside their students, the alliance that develops builds strong connections.

Students at the Bean school actively pursue the opportunity to create videos because the process is fun and exciting. Planning and shooting scenes deepens their understanding of bullying, bystander action, and social norms. Students build feelings of self-efficacy when they realize that their videos will be used to educate others even after they graduate.

At the Bean school we have created videos at all grade levels and on a wide variety of topics. For the purpose of this discussion, I will focus on the legacy videos created by all fifth graders. Legacy videos identify school climate goals and teach younger students effective solutions for social problems. The videos are shared during Peace Day assemblies and used to address specific topics in subsequent years. Planning and creating these videos is a special part of the fifth-grade year and provides students with an opportunity to teach what they have learned over the years and identify what they value about the school. Since all students watch the fifth-grade legacy videos every year, they begin to look forward to creating their own from an early age.

In the beginning, none of us had experience with video editing technology, and so we began with simple, unedited "talking head" interviews, during which students discussed what bullying is, its negative effects on individuals and schools, and what it means for our school to discourage bullying. As we gained experience and skills, we began to create more complex videos with special effects and retakes. We have since experimented with incorporating text on the screen, recording audio and video separately, having a character appear or disappear, and having characters materialize in historic scenes and fantasy locations. I edit the videos and add special effects, but I involve students in editing decisions.

We have structured the process of video creation in many different ways. Based on what has worked best for us, here is a description of our current procedures:

We begin the legacy video process by dividing the fifth grade into small groups—with 10 students being the most productive size. Each group brainstorms a message for their video and techniques for imparting their message to viewers. Often videos follow storylines, but sometimes they consist solely of young people talking about and illustrating their experiences and beliefs. After brainstorming the message and overall structure of the video, we storyboard specific scenes and write a script. The next step is to identify roles and choose people to play them. We have found it effective to devise a random process for choosing roles. We have students draw playing cards from a deck, and the students who draw the highest cards get the first choice of roles. (Allowing students to decide who plays what role is filled with opportunities for rejection and manipulation of social power.)

Next, we shoot scenes. We encourage flexibility, improvisation, and experimentation as we shoot each scene many times. The process of shooting any line of dialogue numerous times while experimenting with pause, emphasis, and wording often helps students feel more comfortable in front of the camera. Creating and viewing different takes of the same scene also help students understand the profound difference in feeling that comes from small changes in inflection and body language.

Fifth graders have created legacy videos based on many topics, among them the following:

- One group of students created a video showing what young people can do when they see someone being mean to someone else.

- Another video showed and discussed how to gain and lose friends.

- During another, students traveled back in time to the moment when Rosa Parks refused to give up her seat on the bus. The students then returned to the present to talk about how they refuse to go along with something wrong in their own lives.

- Finally, another group of students created a video during which a new student comes to the Bean school with two inner voices, one perched on each shoulder.

To provide a concrete example of a legacy video and to illustrate the peer culture of the Bean school, I will describe this last video in detail. The script was written entirely by students, and all roles, including those of adults, were played by students.

Scene 1

As the video begins, the words "At another school . . . far away" scroll across the screen. In the first scene, three boys are playing basketball. The main character, Rebecca, says, "Hi, guys. Can I play?" several times, but the three boys only laugh at her and say, "Yeah, right."

As she walks away with her head down, a girl stops her to say, "I found this flyer," and hands her a piece of paper. Rebecca reads aloud from the flyer:

"The James H. Bean School: Where everybody belongs." Then she asks, "What's this on it?" and points to the bottom half of the flyer.

Voices sing, "F is for friends who do stuff together. U is for you and me. N is for anywhere, anything at all. Here at the James H. Bean."

The girl says, "That's our school song." Rebecca turns to face the camera and says:

"Boy, I wish I was at a school like that." The following words appear on the screen: "And she did move to the Bean school—but she wasn't sure how to act . . ."

Scene 2

Rebecca stands alone during recess. A small head appears to float above her left shoulder. She turns to face this head, and he says to her, "The only way you can show the kids how tough you are is to hurt them. Then everybody will be afraid of you."

This head disappears, and a different head appears to float above her right shoulder.

As Rebecca turns her head to face this second "shoulder person," the head says to her, "Wait a minute, that's no way to make friends. You won't make friends if you're mean."

The left shoulder person appears again to say, "Don't listen to her. Don't be a wimp."

Rebecca turns to face the camera and asks, "Who should I listen to?" She thinks for a minute, then turns to her left shoulder and says, "I think I'll listen to you." Rebecca then walks past a whole line of students and pushes them all out of the way, saying, "Watch out buddies . . . I'm coming through." Then she goes down the slide.

When she's alone again, the left shoulder person appears and says, "That was great. They're going to be so afraid of you."

Rebecca agrees when she says, "Yeah, it's fun."

The right shoulder person cautions Rebecca by saying, "I don't know. They might not like you."

The left shoulder person quickly retorts, "You don't have to listen to her."

Rebecca faces the camera, rubs her hands together, and says again, "This is fun."

Next, Rebecca stands behind a boy using the swing. She says, "Watch out—my turn," as she pushes him off the swing. She gets on the swing and says, "Thank you very much," in a nasty and self-important tone of voice.

The boy Rebecca pushed off the swing approaches a teacher and says, "Mrs. Blackburn, Mrs. Blackburn."

The teacher responds, "Is there a problem?"

The boy replies, "That new kid keeps pushing me."

Another girl on the playground chimes in with, "I saw it, too."

"What happened?" the teacher asks.

"That new girl just came up to him and shoved him off the swing."

"Let me talk to her," the teacher says.

Scene 3

Rebecca is sitting with Mrs. Blackburn at an outdoor picnic table. Mrs. Blackburn asks, "What did you just do?" and Rebecca replies, "Nothing."

Mrs. Blackburn says, "If you did it and you told the truth, your parents would find out that you told the truth."

"I just pushed some little kid off the swing, that's all," Rebecca states.

"Thank you for being honest. We don't allow pushing, hitting, or teasing at our school. I will tell our principal that you pushed. For right now, please sit at this picnic table for the rest of recess," Mrs. Blackburn says.

When Rebecca is alone at the picnic table, she turns to the left shoulder person to say:

"I shouldn't have listened to you."

He replies, "What do you mean?"

The right shoulder person says, "Just be kind to people, okay?" and Rebecca replies, "Okay. Maybe you're right."

Scene 4

Rebecca sits in the principal's office. The principal says:

"Rebecca, I'm the principal, Mr. Cummings. I hear you've done something wrong at recess, and I also hear that you told the truth about what you did."

"I pushed somebody off the swings," Rebecca says.

"Please look at the chart and tell me what your punishment is," the principal requests.

Rebecca reads aloud from the behavior rubric, "Hitting, pushing, slapping, or grabbing: one inside recess, student calls parents."

"How about if you do it again?" the principal asks.

Rebecca replies, "Three inside recesses. Student calls parent."

"That's right. I hope you make better choices tomorrow. Let's call your dad. I'll tell him how great it is that you told the truth," the principal says.

Scene 5

As Mrs. Blackburn says goodbye to Rebecca at the end of the day, she says, "I hope you make a better choice tomorrow."

"I will," Rebecca replies.

Scene 6

The screen fades to black, and a narrator says, "It's the next day, in the gym." In the gym, two boys play. Rebecca stands on the sidelines.

The left shoulder person says to Rebecca, "Push them around. Make them scared of you."

The right shoulder person counters, "No, be kind to them. You don't want to get in trouble again, do you? Besides, you want to make friends."

The left shoulder person argues, "That's foolish. Just push them around." Rebecca approaches the two boys, pushes them down, and takes one of their hats. The boys lie sprawled on the floor while Rebecca leaves the scene.

Mrs. Blackburn enters the scene and helps them up. She asks, "Are you guys okay?"

One boy says, "No, I'm hurt, Mrs. Blackburn."

The other boy adds, "Me, too. Rebecca pushed us down for no reason at all."

The teacher replies, "I'll take her to the principal, Mr. Cummings."

One of the boys says, "Thank you—we want her to stop," and the other adds:

"We want her to be kind so we can be friends with her."

Scene 7

Rebecca stands by herself. The left shoulder person tells her:

"Great work. See, you got that hat," but the right shoulder person counters:

"I don't think that was such a good idea."

Mrs. Blackburn appears in the scene to say, "I saw what you did. We're going to the office. But first give me the hat."

The face of the narrator appears in the screen to say, "The two kids that got hit told the principal what happened. Telling when somebody is mean to you is the right thing to do."

We then see the two boys sitting in the principal's office. "This is the third time she's hit us this week," the first boy states.

The boys fade from the scene, and Rebecca appears in front of the principal. The left shoulder person says to her, "Don't admit to anything," but the right shoulder person counters, "Come on, tell the truth. It'll make you feel better."

Rebecca sighs, looks at the floor, and says, "I've been mean to people since I got here."

The principal responds by saying, "Thank you for telling the truth. That will help you change. Please tell me what your consequence is."

Rebecca glances at the behavior rubric and says, "It looks like I'm in for recess all week."

The principal says, "Remember, it's your choice how you act."

The narrator appears on the screen and says, "She finally started listening to the good advice. Then she could make some friends."

Scene 8

We again see the same two boys playing in the gym. Rebecca approaches them to say, "Guys, I've been mean but I don't want to fight anymore."

The first boy replies, "I like that idea," and the other boy says, "Me, too."

They begin to play a game together, and Rebecca speaks directly to the camera, saying, "And that's how I made friends at the Bean school."

The narrator appears again to say, "And they all lived happily ever after." The screen pans to capture a group of kids playing basketball together. The narrator continues, "Maybe not everybody."

Rebecca's left shoulder person hovers above another student's shoulder, saying, "Hey, you, you can be mean to people."

The student replies, "I don't think so."

The left shoulder person continues, "Then they'll be afraid of you."

The student maintains his position and says, "I don't want people to be afraid of me. I want friends."

Scene 9

Then we see the face of the left shoulder person superimposed in front of a trash can. As many voices say, "Bye-bye," the shoulder person slowly spirals into the trash can and disappears.

To end, the entire video production team stands in front of the camera. In unison, they say:

"Be kind to people, and they'll be kind to you."

As becomes obvious from watching or reading about this video, students at the Bean school clearly understand the disciplinary process, have internalized the messages of the bullying prevention program, and are able to communicate positive messages with sensitivity and honesty. We use this video at the beginning of each year to orient students to school expectations and our discipline system. We also use it to remind them that they can choose positive behavior.

Those interested in using student-created video as a teaching tool need not have experienced shooting or editing digital videos. Requirements are a digital video camera and a computer. I suggest starting with the simplest editing software: iMovie for the Macintosh, or Windows Movie Maker Version 2 for Windows XP. Both are easy to learn and allow the editor to exercise a great deal of creativity. As your skills grow, you can move to more complex editing programs that allow for a wider range of special effects, such as Pinnacle Studio or Ulead Videostudio.

PEACE DAY ASSEMBLIES

The second example of a culture- and norms-based intervention is the Peace Day assembly. I hope the following detailed description of these assemblies includes elements you can implement at your own school. At the Bean school, we have been holding monthly Peace Day assemblies focused on school climate since 2001. The format of these assemblies has evolved over the years, but the goal has always been to help students focus on what they can do, individually and communally, to make the Bean school a great place to learn, grow, and play.

The principal, Nancy Reynolds, and I originally designed Peace Day assemblies to celebrate and reward the improved behavior we observed schoolwide after we began consistently enforcing expectations and discussing bullying with students. In order to craft an assembly format, we looked at the traditions in place at other schools. In some schools we investigated, students who had followed school rules during the previous month attended a reward assembly featuring a performer, video, or some other special event. As we talked with staff at these schools, we realized that it was the same group of students who earned participation in the assemblies each month and came to the conclusion that these assemblies did not act as forces for change. In other schools we observed, assemblies acted as extended classroom meetings and provided students and staff with an opportunity to define and celebrate positive school culture. In these schools, assemblies seemed to create and reinforce positive and expected behaviors. We modeled our first Peace Day assemblies after this latter example. The first Peace Day assemblies were whole-school celebrations during which the principal and counselor pointed out patterns of good behavior and specific positive incidents we had observed during the past month, discussed problems on the playground and in the halls, and welcomed new students and staff. These assemblies were effective in pointing out and reinforcing behavioral expectations but did not allow students to participate in the process of shaping culture.

During the second year, Peace Day assemblies changed in two significant ways. First, the parents' group bought the school a public-address system and wireless handheld microphone. Second, we began to schedule our assemblies by grade level instead of gathering the entire student body. These two changes allowed Peace Day assemblies to become more interactive. We began roaming the audience with microphone in hand and encouraging students to talk about peers who helped them, played with them when they had no one else to play with, and welcomed them when they were new to the school. We started holding discussions about what it means to be a hero and how students could make the Bean school a better place. We talked about bullying and possible bystander interventions. We organized the first of our annual student-initiated food drives. We began airing student-created videos focused on school climate goals, as well as reading and discussing books dealing with justice, fairness, and mutual support. During this stage, Peace Day assemblies focused primarily on recognizing student actions that helped the school community, such as playing with peers who were alone, sticking up for others, and providing emotional support. The assemblies started to become places where students could talk about what social behaviors they valued, their hopes for the school community, and the positive actions they observed in their peers.

From 2003 on, Peace Day assemblies have become even more clearly focused on reflective discussions about school climate. Each monthly assembly now includes some or all of the following five elements:

First, Peace Day assemblies are opportunities to welcome new students and staff. Each new transfer student chooses two peers who have been especially kind. These peers introduce the new student to the rest of the grade and tell the audience why this new student is fun to play with. They also present the new student with a school T-shirt. New students then give feedback to the whole grade level about how others have treated them during their transition to our school.

Second, Peace Day assemblies are times for students to talk about other students' acts of kindness. We ask young people to tell their peers about someone who helped them, reached out in friendship, or showed other positive behavior. The students who exhibited the positive behavior described stand for applause.

Third, we choose a theme and show a video (often student created) or read aloud from a book in order to spark discussion on the theme. These discussions are interactive, and we often bring students to the front to use improvisational theater to experiment with solutions for social problems. They are also topical: During Black History Month, we talk about the history of slavery, discrimination, and African American achievement and discuss what we can apply from the struggle for civil rights to our work striving for a safe and inclusive school environment. During Women's History Month, we discuss gender stereotypes and the importance of inclusion.

Fourth, Peace Day assemblies provide an opportunity for the student council to organize the Thanksgiving food drive, the math-a-thon, and other community service projects.

Finally, we use Peace Day assemblies to have fun and celebrate with songs, silly books, talent shows, and other student-created activities.

Starting in 2005, based on a teacher's suggestion, we added another element to Peace Day assemblies. In the beginning of the school year, each grade level began to choose a goal for the year and brainstorm strategies to meet this goal. Throughout the year, we continue to discuss their goals, monitor progress, and brainstorm new strategies. Following are the goals and strategies students set for the 2005–2006 school year, provided as an example of the kinds of goals young people are capable of implementing.

Kindergarten and first-grade goal for the year: We want everyone to have friends.

How we will make this happen:

> We will ask people to play with us.
>
> We will play with people.
>
> We will look around and make sure no one is left out.
>
> When someone doesn't want to play, we will ask him or her again another day.
>
> We will smile and say hello to people.

Second- and third-grade goal for the year: We want no name-calling or teasing.

How we will make this happen:

> If our friends are calling people names, we will ask our friends nicely to stop.
>
> If peers are being called names, we will help them get away.
>
> If others call us names, we will get away from them or ask for help.
>
> If we are thinking about calling someone else a name, we will count to 10 or take a breath and think about what we are going to say before we say it.

Fourth-grade goals for the year: We want people to play by the rules and be fair. When work is hard, we want to remember to work harder instead of giving up.

How we will make this happen:

> We will remember that when we win by cheating, we feel bad later.
>
> We will remember not to complain when we are losing, but to try harder instead.
>
> We will remember that we feel bad about ourselves when we give up on schoolwork right away.
>
> When something is hard, we will keep trying.
>
> We will remember that if we keep trying, most of the time we will be able to achieve success.
>
> We will remember that even when we fail, at least we will know that we tried.
>
> We will remember that if we copy someone else's work and call it our own, we will feel bad later.

Fifth-grade goals for the year: We do not want to have a popular group, with others left out. When work is hard, we want to remember to work harder instead of giving up.

How we will achieve this:

> When someone tries to start a popular group, we will not go along with that person.
>
> We will play with everyone and include those who are left out.
>
> We will stick up for people when others are leaving them out.
>
> When our peers are mean, we will ask them to stop in a nice way.
>
> We will help others get away if they are being teased.
>
> We won't give others too much power by going along with them if they say things such as "I will only be your friend if you . . ." We will reply, "No, thanks."

We will remember that we feel proud when we try harder when work is difficult and don't feel proud of ourselves when we give up.

❦

Follow-up discussions focused on these grade-level goals follow the same format as follow-up discussions for classroom lessons on social problem solving. Throughout the year we ask a number of open-ended questions focused on helping students assess their progress toward meeting their goals and fine-tuning their strategies. Possible questions include

"Who used this strategy?"

"Did it work?"

"Do we need to change or modify our strategies to meet our goal?"

"Are we getting closer to our goal?"

"How can you tell?"

We also follow up on school-climate goals during informal conversations in classrooms, halls, and on the playground. We inform parents of the grade-level goals through the parent newsletter and encourage them to discuss and reinforce these goals with their children.

Up to this point, I have discussed the changes over the years in the format and content of Peace Day assemblies. There has also been a subtle yet important change in feeling about them. Our first assemblies were didactic and adult-directed. The principal and I chose specific messages to impart each month. With the introduction of the wireless microphone and student-created video, we were able to begin a transition from adult-directed to student-directed assemblies. Increasingly, Peace Day assemblies are safe places for adults to ask open-ended questions and sit back to allow students to discuss with and teach each other. Students teach each other problem-solving solutions through video and live demonstrations. Students brainstorm and vote on goals and evaluate their progress toward meeting those goals throughout the year. Students now often move the microphone around the audience themselves, turning Peace Day assemblies into forums to discuss their visions for the Bean school. As Peace Day assemblies have become collaborations between staff and students, rather than a series of adult-directed activities, students have learned to take ownership of school climate and take pride for positive change.

SUMMARY AND CONCLUSIONS

When I recently asked a fourth-grade class what is special about our school, one student said, without prompting, "We take time to talk about what is important and how we do things at this school, like in Peace Days." These monthly assemblies provide the entire school community with an opportunity to reflect on and consciously shape school culture. Interventions such as student-created videos and Peace Day assemblies give students an active voice in shaping school culture. Over time, these interventions can empower young people to work with adults as full partners in our efforts to make schools safe and inclusive. Actively involving students and explicitly discussing school culture deepens bullying prevention programs and encourages young people to become empathetic, self-confident, and active citizens.

Afterword

Building Future Citizens

Although it is clear that many factors shape young people, the school environment certainly helps determine how students will think and act as adults. While I know of no research about the long-term effects of bullying prevention programs, I believe successful and widespread bullying prevention programs have the potential to create a generation of empathetic, self-confident adults who are willing to act against injustice. Based on the changes I have seen in students at the Bean school during our eight years' implementing a comprehensive bullying prevention program, the following outcomes are what I see as the potential long-standing legacy of bullying prevention.

Students develop a strong understanding of and appreciation for justice, honesty, and fair treatment for all.

Students at the Bean school believe that wrongs can be righted. They see that adults support and protect those needing protection, treat all students fairly, and do not judge or stereotype students. Students believe that honesty leads to justice and know that telling the truth about their own misbehavior will lead to fair consequences and assistance in changing their behavior. They feel comfortable asking adults for help and are confident that they will get help when they need it. Our students are outraged when they hear about young people who are not allowed to go to school, segregation, the Holocaust, and other injustices. When this outrage is combined with knowledge, skills, and a sense of self-efficacy, students learn to act in the face of injustice. I believe that our students will grow up to be adults who expect fairness and honesty in relationships, at work, from businesses, and from the government. They will make themselves heard if they experience or observe injustice.

Students develop a strong drive to help others, and they value and include their peers.

Young people at the Bean school speak up for others, join together to seek out and play with isolated peers, insist that adults use fair methods of choosing classroom volunteers, mentor younger students, and raise money for needy people, both in their own community and in other parts of the world. Although in the beginning these activities were primarily initiated by adults, they are now student initiated. For example, in early 2007 our fifth-grade students developed a tutoring program. They decided that fifth-grade volunteers would give up one recess a week to help struggling younger writers. During the first recruiting meeting, one third of the fifth-grade class signed up. By working to teach empathy, we encourage students to understand, respect, and care for their peers. Students act on their feelings of empathy because they feel safe and supported by a school culture that values inclusion and helpfulness. I believe our students are likely to become adults who volunteer, choose helping professions, and reach out to marginalized and excluded populations.

Students who are naturally gifted and popular learn not to abuse their power.

At the Bean school, as at every school I have worked in or visited, there are students with exceptional gifts, attractiveness, confidence, charm, and family support. These students' peers naturally admire them. At the Bean school, these students sometimes attempt to use their popularity to control others and gain power. Most years, a subgroup of popular students emerges and begins to manipulate peers by telling them they will be their friends only if they act in certain ways. Targets of this manipulative behavior rarely allow popular students to gain and abuse power. All students have learned to react to attempts to manipulate by quietly refusing to be controlled and choosing friends who do not try to control them. Students know that adults will support and protect them if their peers escalate their abuse of power to the level of exclusion, name-calling, rumors, or other aggression. When popular students' attempts to gain power are ineffective, they can instead learn to enjoy honest friendship, real connections, and earned achievements. I believe our students will become adults who use power responsibly and do not allow others to manipulate them.

Student bystanders act to help targets instead of passively observing or encouraging bullying.

Students at the Bean school learn, practice, and use a wide range of safe and effective actions when they see someone calling names, excluding, starting rumors, or hitting. They tell adults what they see and hear. They help targets get away and support targets later. They notice and point out positive changes in the behavior of aggressive youth. They take pride in protecting peers and feel safe knowing that others will support and protect them. I believe our students will become adult citizens who stand up for others and act in the face of harassment and aggression.

Students develop a strong sense of self-efficacy.

Students at the Bean school know their actions make a difference. They set, work toward, and attain goals. They know they have many solutions to choose from when faced with problems. They see how, as individuals, they make their school a better place for themselves and others. This sense of possibility leads students to be creative and initiate new interventions to improve school culture. I believe our students will become empowered citizens who see and use their ability to create positive change.

As I touched on in the introduction, bullying is intimately related to other abuses of power. Working to empower students to prevent bullying is connected to all work to create just, honest, and inclusive communities. As I look toward the future, I can see our students having significant positive impacts on the world.

Appendix A

Scope and Sequence of the James H. Bean Elementary School Guidance Program

At the Bean school, we have worked to create a comprehensive guidance program based on our community's needs, using a sequential teaching approach for social and emotional skills, student motivation, and bystander action. Our hope is that all of our students will learn to be active learners and involved citizens. Our current outline is presented here in the hope that you will find parts of it useful.

OBJECTIVES

1. To build students' skills in identifying and distinguishing between different types of peer problems.

2. To build students' skills in generating many solutions for problems and choosing from among those solutions.

3. To build students' skills in making friends and including all classmates.

4. To build students' listening skills and ability to accept that they won't always get their way.

5. To build students' skills in supporting and protecting peers.

6. To encourage students to tell adults about problems with peers that they cannot solve themselves.

7. To build students' knowledge of their own and others' feelings and techniques to express and cope with feelings.

8. To build students' abilities to regulate their feelings, body movement, and activity level and to use their bodies in safe and respectful ways.

9. To build students' awareness of respectful and disrespectful communication with peers and adults.

10. To build students' respect for diversity.

11. To help students appreciate, understand, and build on their own unique temperaments and interests.

12. To connect students' likes, dislikes, and goals with different career choices.

13. To build students' internal motivation for learning.

14. To build students' abilities to prevent and deal with peer-to-peer problems, such as exclusion, rumors, and the abuse of popularity.

15. To incorporate the following values into daily school life: full accountability for one's own actions, honesty, and inclusion.

ACTIVITIES

1. Weekly 30-minute classroom guidance meetings during one trimester each year. These sessions can be extended beyond the trimester, if necessary.

2. Monthly grade-level Peace Day assemblies. These assemblies focus on positive actions within the school community and student-set goals for the school year.

3. Weekly meetings with all fifth-grade students during the second half of the year to plan and create legacy videos, which give students a voice to teach younger peers about the positive social norms of the school and techniques for positive interaction.

4. Student council activities to reinforce these objectives.

5. Informal and formal counseling and mentoring by staff.

6. In-the-moment staff interventions to reinforce established language and skills.

Topics for Weekly Classroom Guidance Meetings

We concentrate on topics geared toward the developmental needs of each age group and the needs of our particular community of students. We focus on other topics according to the needs of a particular class or events within the school or in the wider community.

Kindergarten

- No means no.
- Acceptance of not always getting what one wants.
- Listening to adults when told to change activities.
- Naming and recognizing feelings.
- Self-calming and self-control through breathing and other techniques.
- The importance of including and playing with everyone.
- Welcoming individual differences.

First grade

- Review of lessons learned in kindergarten.
- Hands are for helping, not hurting.
- Using kind words and actions.
- Responsibility for one's actions.
- Listening.

Second grade

- Concepts and skills for problem solving.
- Identifying peer problems.
- Differentiating between small problems and large problems.
- Dealing with small problems themselves and telling adults about large problems.

- Generating a wide range of solutions to social problems and learning which solutions work well with which problems.

Third grade

- Strategies for supporting and protecting peers dealing with exclusion or bullying.
- How to include isolated youth.
- How and when to tell adults when observing unkind behavior.
- Eleanor Estes's book *The Hundred Dresses* (Harcourt, 2004/1944).

Fourth grade

- Skills for collaboration.
- Internal motivation for academic work.
- Work done for the sake of learning and mastery is more enjoyable than work done to comply with adult demands.
- Appreciation for individual differences, including goals and temperaments.
- Career awareness.

Fifth grade

- Preventing rumors, exclusion, and relational aggression.
- The dynamics of friendship.
- Defining and creating positive peer culture schoolwide.
- Being mentors, leaders, and teachers to younger students.

The Hundred Dresses: A Series of Lessons Focusing on Bystander Action

I have found that literature, and Eleanor Estes's book *The Hundred Dresses* (2004 / 1944) in particular, is a powerful tool that can stimulate discussion about bystander action in bullying situations. This appendix includes a series of lessons that demonstrate ways to use literature in bullying prevention. The techniques presented in these lessons would be useful in helping students learn from many other books as well. I encourage you to use them as a springboard from which to launch your own literature-based work with students.

The Hundred Dresses, set in the 1940s, tells the story of Wanda, Peggy, and Maddie. Maddie and Peggy are best friends. Peggy teases Wanda, who is a social outcast. Maddie feels uncomfortable with her friend's bullying behavior and guilty about her inaction. Maddie never has the opportunity to make things right with Wanda, which surprises students, who expect the book to have a happy ending. Maddie's feelings of guilt have great power with young people. In order for students to experience the most profound impact, we can strive not to give away the ending. As the story gradually unfolds, students receive the key message slowly: If you do not act against injustice when you have the chance, it may become too late to make a difference. Specific and concrete descriptions of the characters' words and body language provide rich opportunities for students to build empathy through reenacting scenes. This book is especially useful for teaching empathy and helping bystanders move toward safe and effective action.

I teach these lessons to third graders at the Bean school, but I believe they would also be effective up to fifth grade. I typically dedicate 10 to 12 half-hour classroom guidance sessions to these lessons. The format of the classroom discussions depends somewhat on the learning styles and needs of each particular class. Some groups are more productive in their seats, whereas others work best when sitting on a rug. Some groups require more structure than others. With all groups, I have found it helpful to follow predictable and enjoyable welcome and ending rituals. I end each lesson with a magic trick to leave the class with a pleasant feeling of anticipation for the next session. A trick, a song, or a brainteaser at the end of the lesson provides incentive for students to settle down and focus, as those who are disruptive may miss that predictable reward.

My basic format for the lessons is to read the book aloud, stopping periodically to discuss or act out specific scenes. It is important to strike a balance between letting the story unfold and stopping to clarify and deepen discussion and activities. Sometimes, discussions should be brief so students won't lose the flow of the story. At other times, we should depart from the story for long periods of time, but make sure to repeatedly review the plot and what we know about the characters when we return to the book. We should continually attempt to connect the story to students' own lives, thus deepening their understanding of topics discussed and making real action more likely. We should gauge our audience and spend more or less time on any given topic or theme, depending on their needs and interests. This flexibility allows us to customize lessons to each class. In the following pages I will lay out a series of 10 lessons based on *The Hundred Dresses,* but I encourage you to change, shorten, or extend each topic, depending on your goals and student interest.

SESSION ONE: CHAPTER 1

During the first class period, I begin by talking about how much I love the book. I show some of the artwork and ask students what they think. I tell students that the book was first published in 1944, before most of their grandparents were born. I ask them if they think there will be differences between the lives of children in the book and their own lives. We brainstorm a list of the possible differences, and I write them on the board. I ask students to raise their hands when they hear aspects of the children's lives they recognize as different from their own.

I start reading the first chapter but stop after the second sentence: "But nobody, not even Peggy and Madeline, the girls who started all the fun, noticed her absence." I ask the class what the word *fun* means, and I list their answers on the board. In the second paragraph, I stop after the sentence "She sat in the corner of the room where the rough boys who did not make good marks on their report cards sat." Students will often recognize this difference between schools of the 1940s and today's schools. I ask the class how they think it would affect students with low motivation or difficulty learning to be placed in the back of the room and ignored, and we talk about 1940s schools as sorting machines, where students who struggled academically were excluded, ignored, and encouraged to quit school and work instead. I ask if the students who do not get good grades sit in the back corner of their classroom. They respond that students who struggle are more likely to sit in front so they can get extra help from the teacher. This historical theme, and an ensuing discussion touching on fairness, help to foreshadow Wanda's social exclusion.

As the chapter describes Wanda's home and neighborhood, I continue to ask questions to connect the book to students' own lives. For example, I ask if any students live on dirt roads or at the end of muddy driveways. In the fourth paragraph, I stop after the following line: "But no one really thought much about Wanda Petronski once she was in the classroom. The time they thought about her was outside of school hours, at noon-time when they were coming back to school, or in the morning early before school hours." I point out that in the 1940s children walked home for lunch. This can act as a segue into a further discussion of ways in which children's lives differed from the 1940s to the present day. After this discussion, I reread the previous paragraph in order to regain continuity, and then I stop again after the sentence "Then sometimes they waited for Wanda—to have fun with her." I ask the class what the difference is between "having fun with" somebody and "making fun of" somebody. We look at these two very different meanings of the word *fun* and brainstorm examples of each definition. I ask the students which definition they think the author of the book implies.

On the following page, we begin to learn about the other main characters—Peggy and Maddie—although at this point descriptions are superficial. Students will often make premature judgments of Peggy, based on her appearance, but I remind them that we can't tell yet what kind of person she really is. I stop after the sentence "The reason Peggy and Maddie noticed Wanda's absence was because Wanda had made them late to school." I ask the class how Wanda could have made them late for school, given that Wanda was absent that day. We receive the answer in the following sentence: "They had waited and waited for Wanda—to have some fun with her—and she just hadn't come . . . finally they had to race off without seeing her." I ask the students if Wanda really made them late to school. This question leads to a discussion of the difference between actually being made to do something and just saying that we are made to do something when we really had a choice. Students often distinguish between these two situations by calling one category *reasons* and the other *excuses.* I ask them to brainstorm examples of reasons and excuses from their own lives. For many of the examples, I push students to describe how they felt after using excuses, and how adults and peers reacted. I often broaden this discussion to talk about the various meanings of the word *because.*

I end the first session by asking the students to summarize the story so far and predict what will happen next.

SESSION TWO: CHAPTER 2 (FIRST HALF)

I begin the second class session by discussing the title of chapter 2: "The Dresses Game." I ask students to brainstorm several short definitions of *game* and write them on the board. I begin to read aloud but stop after the sentence "They often waited for Wanda Petronski—to have fun with her." I remind the class of our previously determined definitions of the word *fun* and ask them why the phrase "have fun with her" keeps appearing in the book.

I continue to read as the book describes life in Boggins Heights, where Wanda lives. I show the class the illustration of Mr. Svenson's house and ask them to imagine what Wanda's house might look like. I ask students specific questions about what they think it would be like to live in houses such as these. For example, I ask them how much room there would be inside and what would happen during a snowstorm. I stop reading again after the paragraph that begins "Wanda Petronski. Most of the children in Room 13 didn't have names like that. They had names easy to say." I take this opportunity to start a discussion about diversity and individual differences. Since I work with students in rural Maine, which generally lacks ethnic diversity, I ask them what it would be like to go to a school where students come from many different cultures. I ask students what kinds of diversity exist in our school. Discussions about diversity will vary from school to school, but the goal should be to help students see how knowing others who are different from them can enrich their lives. I read again until the line "Wanda didn't have any friends. She came to school alone and went home alone." I ask the class how it would feel to have no friends and how Wanda could lack friends when everyone always seems to be "having fun with her." As the paragraph describes her one worn dress, I point out that girls were forced to wear dresses in the 1940s. Sometimes students don't believe me. I respect their disbelief but am prepared with personal stories from my own and my mother's past to substantiate my statement. I ask the girls in the class how their lives would be different if they were not allowed to wear pants to school. I ask them how it would affect recess and what it would be like in the winter.

Soon the book describes how Peggy teases Wanda. After reading the dialogue on pages 12 and 13, I put the book aside so students can act out the dialogue and actions described in the book. By mimicking the dialogue and stage directions described in the book, students often gain a deeper understanding of how the characters feel. I learned this technique from the mime and teacher Tony Montanaro, who wrote, "When an actor/mime is uncertain of a character's temperament, it is often helpful to assume a body position that the character would take" (1995, p. 29). To help students open up to the idea of acting, I set clear boundaries for emotional safety, emphasize fun, and frequently praise the actors. I allow all students the opportunity to act. When I ask students to repeat scenes with further stage directions, I avoid criticizing them by pretending we are shooting a movie and using the phrase "Take two!" instead of emphasizing what they did wrong. I devise a random method for choosing volunteers, and when boys are called upon to play girls' roles, I allow them to change names and topics of conversation when necessary. After each version of any scene, I ask the student actors how they felt in the roles they played.

First, I focus on how Peggy feels when she teases Wanda. I ask one student to perform the following scene, repeating Peggy's line in a taunting manner: " 'Wanda,' she'd say, giving one of her friends a nudge, 'tell us. How many dresses did you say you had hanging up in your closet?' " As students take turns acting out this scene, I ask them how it feels to act like Peggy. In the beginning, I often need to prompt students to identify feelings, as opposed to thoughts. I accept answers such as "She thinks Wanda is no good" or "She thinks she's the ice cream sundae with the cherry on top," but I follow these answers by pushing students to also provide feeling statements, such as "She feels powerful" or "She feels admired." Next, we explore Wanda's reaction to Peggy's question, as described in the following quote: " 'Yeah, a hundred, all lined up,' said Wanda. Then her thin lips drew together in silence." I show the class how to draw their thin lips together in silence and let them sit in this position in silence for a minute. I ask them how it feels to hold their lips that way and how they think Wanda feels. Next, I randomly choose pairs of students to act out the entire exchange between Peggy and Wanda on pages 12 and 13, during which Peggy makes fun of Wanda's statement that she has a hundred dresses at home. During this process, I teach students what the word *stolidly* means. I encourage animation and perkiness in those playing the role of Peggy, and thin-lipped, monotone speech in those playing the role of Wanda. I demonstrate and encourage students to practice different ways of standing for the two characters. As Peggy, I stand tall and confidently, with my shoulders back and head held high. As Wanda, I round my shoulders forward, as if protecting my core. As students take on the body postures of the characters, they become better able to identify the characters' feelings.

I begin reading again, but stop after the line "Then they'd let her go. And then before she'd gone very far, they couldn't help bursting into shrieks and peals of laughter." I point out the phrase "they *couldn't help* bursting into . . . laughter" and ask the class what this means. I ask them if this reminds them of anything they've already heard in the book. This is a good time to review the reason versus excuse discussion from the previous session. We focus not only on why characters in the book make excuses, but also on students' own lives. I ask them when they have used excuses, how they felt, and how others reacted.

I stop reading again after the line "And the girls laughed derisively, while Wanda moved over to the . . . wall of the school building where she usually stood and waited for the bell to ring." Again, I choose students to act out the scene and ask them afterward how they felt while they played the various roles. I continue reading until the following page, which describes yet another incident of teasing. After reading the line "Wanda would shift her eyes quickly from Peggy to a distant spot, as though she were looking far ahead, looking but not seeing anything," I demonstrate this type of stare. The entire class and I practice the stare together, and again I ask them what they have learned about Wanda's feelings by acting like her. I continue to read, stopping to point out when the teasing is again referred to as a game and returning to our discussion from the beginning of the session. In the same paragraph comes perhaps the most powerful event in the book: "And finally Wanda would move up the street, her eyes dull and her mouth closed tight, hitching her left shoulder every now and then in the funny way she had, finishing the walk to school alone." I enlist students to act out this scene to discover how Wanda feels.

Given the wealth of powerful material found in chapter 2, I rarely make it past this section. Wherever I choose to stop, I leave time to summarize the session by asking the following three questions: "What happened in this chapter?" "What do we know about each character?" and "What do you think will happen next?" I praise the students for their willingness to act, then reinforce that we act in order to understand others' feelings.

SESSION THREE: CHAPTER 2 (SECOND HALF)

After briefly reviewing our work from the first two sessions, I begin the third class session by discussing the paragraph in chapter 2 that begins "Peggy was not really cruel." I ask students what this phrase means, given how Peggy behaves toward Wanda.

In the next paragraph, we finally begin to learn more about Maddie. When having students act out the following scene, I focus their attention primarily on how Maddie feels: "Sometimes when Peggy was asking Wanda those questions in that mock polite voice, Maddie felt embarrassed and studied the marbles in the palm of her hand, rolling them around and saying nothing herself." I often read without stopping for the rest of the chapter to help students get caught up in the flow of the story.

When I finish reading the second chapter, I often have time left in the third class session to review in detail what we know about each character, anticipate what will happen next, and discuss parallel behaviors they observe at our school. I remind students not to use names or otherwise identify individuals during this discussion. At this point, I often introduce the idea of a "Maddie moment," which was invented by a Bean school third grader. He described a Maddie moment as a time when one observes an act of cruelty and wants to stop it but is afraid and doesn't know what action to take. I point out that adults have Maddie moments, too, and we create a list on the board of Maddie moments we have experienced. I keep this list to spark discussion during following class sessions.

SESSION FOUR: SKILL PRACTICE

I abandon the book during the fourth class session to focus on discovering effective solutions for Maddie's dilemma with improvisational theater. I begin the class by quickly reviewing the plot and what we know about the characters. We then return to the scenes of teasing from the second chapter, and as students act them out again, I push them to figure out what Maddie could have done differently. I encourage the students playing Maddie to ask the audience for help. When audience members have ideas, they raise their hands. The actors call on them and experiment with their ideas in the scene. Each group of actors repeats the scene several times, using different solutions each time, before they allow three more students to assume the roles of Peggy, Maddie, and Wanda. Throughout the process, I encourage actors to act as naturally as possible and to keep in mind what they know about the characters as people.

When supervising this process, it is essential to strike a balance between encouraging creativity and discouraging damaging solutions. When students propose solutions we find unlikely to be effective but will not worsen the situation, we can allow them to discover the effectiveness or ineffectiveness of the proposed solutions through practice and discussion. When students propose solutions likely to make the situation worse, such as for Maddie to punch Peggy, I remind students that these kinds of solutions are not allowed at our school. Students should not practice destructive solutions. Students will often suggest that Maddie directly confront Peggy. As I discussed earlier in this book, I believe we should discourage confrontation in order to make room for more realistic solutions. To make this point with students, I ask them about the positive and negative aspects of direct confrontation and how likely Maddie would be to confront her friend directly. Maddie is, in many ways, a perfect example of the difficulties of confrontation because her fear of the consequences of this action prevents her from doing anything. Because she is focused on confrontation as the only solution to her problem, she never considers playing with Wanda, telling a teacher, telling her parents, or distracting Peggy by offering another game to play, all of which would have been likely to help. Students will also suggest actions for Wanda to take. When they recommend that Wanda "just walk away" and students practice this solution, I ask if this is easy or difficult. Students often find that turning their backs on Peggy while she is teasing them feels as though it indicates vulnerability and failure. When students suggest that Wanda stand up for herself by telling Peggy how she feels, I ask how likely it is that Peggy and her peers will listen to anything Wanda has to say. They often reply that it is unlikely. We talk about Wanda's positive options, including telling adults and arriving at school later, while emphasizing that Wanda needs help from others.

After using improvisational theater to discover alternative solutions to Maddie's dilemma in chapter 2, I ask students to describe Maddie moments in their own lives. As always, I instruct them to leave out names of aggressors and targets, but otherwise I push for a great deal of detail. Groups of actors then experiment with these real-life scenarios and practice different solutions. Throughout this process, we maintain a list of solutions on the board, continually rate their effectiveness, and fine-tune the list. Before the end of the fourth session, I give students the following homework: to use some of the bystander solutions we came up with during the following week and record their effectiveness.

SESSION FIVE: MORE SKILL PRACTICE

During the fifth class session, I depart yet again from the book and instead focus on the responses to their homework. I write their list of solutions from the previous session on the board and ask students who tried the first solution to identify themselves. For each individual who tried the solution, I write a "+" next to the solution if they report that it worked, a "?" if they report that it made the situation neither better nor worse, and a " - " next to the solution if they report that it made the situation worse. I repeat this process for each of our listed solutions. I often find that a solution will receive all three types of marks. I ask students what this means and help them understand that different situations call for different solutions. We also discuss subtle factors that impact the effectiveness of solutions, such as tone of voice, facial expression, and proximity. As we deepen our discussion, we fine-tune solutions and break them into subcategories. For example, bystanders can help targets escape bullying by asking them, from close proximity or from a distance, depending on how safe bystanders feel, to come and play with them. We summarize the fifth session by reviewing the plot of the book and what we have learned so far.

SESSION SIX: CHAPTER 3

For the sixth class session, I return to the book. Before beginning to read, I review by asking students what has happened in the book so far and what we know about each character. I build anticipation by telling students that they are finally going to learn how the "game" started.

The beginning of the chapter provides more information about Maddie. I stop after the line "Wanda's desk, though empty, seemed to be the only thing [Maddie] saw when she looked over to that side of the room." I ask the class what this tells us about Maddie as a person. I also question students about the line "Afterwards it didn't seem like bright blue weather anymore, although the weather had not changed in the slightest." I strive to read the remainder of the chapter with few interruptions, in order to immerse the class in the unfolding story. After finishing the chapter, I return to the description that begins on page 24 of how Wanda approaches the group of girls. I encourage students to experiment with walking like Wanda, in order to discover how she feels before the teasing begins. I continue to question students about why Wanda feels the way she does and use this scene to lead into a discussion of the profound negative impacts of exclusion. I continue to read the chapter aloud for the second time, stopping to highlight several sentences, such as when Maddie is relieved to hear the school bell. I finish the session with a discussion of the following sentence: "It all happened so suddenly and unexpectedly, with everybody falling right in, that even if you felt uncomfortable as Maddie had there wasn't anything you could do about it." I ask the class if this statement is true. If they say no, I ask why Maddie would say this to herself. I ask students to summarize what they have learned so far and predict what will happen next.

SESSION SEVEN: CHAPTER 4

I begin the seventh class session by discussing the Maddie moments students have experienced during the past week. For each moment described, I ask the following questions: "What happened?" "What were you thinking?" "What did you do?" and "What will you do next time?"

I start reading chapter 4 and stop after the phrase "Maddie was glad she had not *had to* make fun of Wanda." I talk with students about how we cannot only make excuses, but also talk ourselves into believing them. I ask how Maddie limits herself by making excuses and what happens when we say, "They made me do it," when we really choose our own behavior. I continue to read until page 36 before reviewing the statements Maddie makes to herself—namely, that "she'd never have the courage to speak right out to Peggy," "Peggy could not possibly do anything really wrong," and Maddie "was just some girl who lived up on Boggins Heights and stood alone in the school yard." Maddie's thoughts provide much useful material for discussion. I ask the class why Maddie is dishonest with herself and what they think she should say to herself.

I begin reading again and stop after the sentence "For girls, this contest consisted of designing dresses, and for boys, of designing motor boats." This line stimulates discussion about gender-role inflexibility in the 1940s. I ask students how they would feel if told that only girls could cook or only boys could climb trees. Once I introduce the idea of the limitations of gender roles, I can ask students about the differing expectations placed on girls and boys today. During this discussion, I strive to focus on how they feel about gender-based limitations for boys and girls and how to avoid limiting others by allowing them to move beyond typical gender roles.

SESSION EIGHT: CHAPTERS 5 AND 6

I begin the eighth session with the same review with which I start other lessons: I ask students to summarize the story, what we know about each character, and their own Maddie moments. I begin to read chapter 5 until I arrive at the letter from Wanda's father on page 47. I read this letter slowly and deliberately, following stage directions as if I am the teacher. I pause after finishing the letter to let reality sink in. I ask students how they feel and what might happen next. For a short time, I let them fantasize that Wanda's father will change his mind, Maddie will move to Wanda's new school, or Maddie will see Wanda one last time before she moves. I read chapter 6 dramatically and with few pauses for discussion or acting. Throughout the chapter, I do continually ask the class if Peggy understands that she hurt Wanda. In the book, the answer to this question is unclear, which opens avenues for discussion. We discuss how aggressive youth may or may not develop empathy, and if they do not, they are likely to continue their hurtful behavior. I ask students what these young people's lives will be like if they do or don't learn to care about and be kind to others. Through this conversation, I strive to help students develop empathy for bullies while maintaining accountability.

I often stop reading aloud from the book at the end of chapter 6. The remainder of the book, in my view, takes away from instead of adding to the impact and message. When I end with chapter 6, I end with Maddie's epiphany: "She was never going to stand by and say nothing again." I emphasize to students that Maddie will never get the chance to help Wanda. I then ask students what realizations and decisions they have come to as a result of listening to the story. To end, I return to our discussion of our own Maddie moments and the solutions we have developed to deal with them.

SESSIONS NINE AND TEN: LEARNING THROUGH TEACHING OTHERS

I spend the ninth and tenth class sessions helping students devise ways to teach younger students what they have learned. I allow students to choose their own methods, which can range from making posters or presenting at assemblies to making videos. During the 2005–2006 school year, the Bean school third graders chose to make videos. One group performed a literal retelling of the story and then talked on camera about how they felt about the story and what they learned. A second group retold the story with an alternate ending. In their telling of the story, Maddie helped Wanda get away from Peggy, and then Maddie and Wanda played together. The third group chose to mention the story briefly before discussing their own solutions to their own Maddie moments. Methods for students to teach are endless. What is important is that students are meaningfully involved in teaching others—thus sharing information, making their school a better place, and deepening their own learning.

First, Do No Harm: A Lesson to Reduce Relational Aggression

This lesson, which is geared toward third to fifth graders, was developed and implemented by staff at the Bean school after a conflict between two friends in the fourth grade escalated into a class-wide war. One of the friends threw a party and did not invite the other, even though they had been close friends. The friend who threw the party did not tell the other student about the party in advance but instead called her from the party. During the ensuing conflict, other students who were previously friendly with both of these children took sides and began to fight with their own friends, according to whose side they were taking. Students who were not especially friendly with either student jumped into the conflict: spreading rumors, telling other people whose side they were on, and turning the school into a nonstop conflict zone. This or a similar lesson could grow out of a like incident in your school or might be planned in anticipation of common behavior patterns.

To begin the lesson, I draw a circle on the board and write the letters A and B inside the circle. I tell the students that A and B are friends but that A did something mean to B—for example, not inviting B to a party, making fun of B, or starting a rumor about B. I ask the class, "What can B do?" We brainstorm ideas and consider the possible consequences of each solution. Students often tell me that B could do something mean to A, either directly or indirectly. This, they tell me, is likely to lead to a bigger fight. They also tell me that B could ask A to stop the hurtful behavior. I ask how many times B will ask A to stop before giving up on the friendship. Students tell me that the number of attempts someone would make would depend on the depth of the friendship and that they would not accept mean behavior from a friend forever. They add that A may or may not listen to B. Another option is for B to play with someone else. If B decides to play with someone else, B can choose later to return to playing with A or continue to play with others. Students tell me that B could also tell a teacher about A's behavior. I ask students what factors will influence B's actions. They reply that it depends on how much fun A and B used to have together, how many times A has been mean to B, and how hurtful the behavior was. At the end of our discussion, it appears that B has several potentially effective solutions to choose from.

I proceed by stating that conflict between friends is rarely a simple matter of A and B. Real-life scenarios are more complicated because others inevitably become involved. I add three additional circles to my drawing to illustrate the complexity of conflict within groups, as the figure shows. I ask students to describe when they have seen peers become involved in a conflict between two individuals. We divide peers into three groups, depending on their proximity to the conflict. I write the letters C, D, and E inside the circle closest to A and B's middle circle. I explain to the class that individuals C through E are close friends of A's and B's. As I write the letters F, G, and H in the next circle outward, I explain that these individuals observed A's behavior but are not close friends of A's or B's. Finally, I write the letters I, J, K, and L in the outer circle and explain that these individuals only heard about A's behavior.

After acknowledging the complexity of conflict in peer groups, I move on to introduce the principle "First, do no harm." We begin by talking about this principle as it applies to medicine and education. When I question students about this principle, they reply that doctors and teachers should, first and foremost, ensure that they don't make a problem worse. To apply the principle to peer conflict, I first ask how A's and B's close friends (C through E) could worsen the conflict. Students answer that they could make the situation worse by taking sides, starting rumors, telling other students what A did, telling A and B they have to be friends again before they are ready to

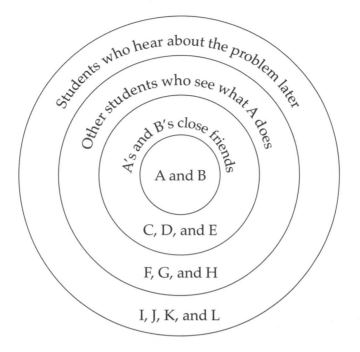

Students who hear about the problem later

Other students who see what A does

A's and B's close friends

A and B

C, D, and E

F, G, and H

I, J, K, and L

reconcile, picking on A or B, or inciting A and B to fight. Next, I ask the class how individuals F through H could make the conflict worse. They reply that these individuals could worsen the situation by starting or passing on rumors, picking on A or B, or laughing at the conflict. Last, we discuss how individuals I through L could make the conflict worse. Students tell me that the students most removed from the conflict could have a negative impact by joining the conflict: spreading rumors or taking sides and starting to fight with those who choose the opposite side. I ask students what negative impacts the previously brainstormed behaviors can have on a conflict between friends. They reply that when others join the conflict, B may hear lies about what A said or did and retaliate, or A may get in trouble for something he or she didn't do, thus leading to arguments between parents and teachers. What began as a small conflict can grow, which makes it harder for B to choose and enact an effective solution.

My next questions focus on why students C through L might behave in ways that worsen the conflict between A and B. I ask the class what goals and needs these individuals are trying to meet. Some possible reasons to get involved are to make their lives more exciting or more like television shows. Students talk about how people may get involved to feel powerful. Others talk about wanting to help A and B get back together so they would not have to choose between them as friends.

Finally, we discuss what C through L could do to improve the conflict. The first step for these individuals is to avoid the behaviors that make the situation worse. Students also tell me that C through L could play with A and B separately, refuse to spread rumors or talk to A or B about the other one, tell a teacher if they are concerned for another's physical or emotional safety, refuse to be controlled if A or B tells them not to play with the other one, or stay out of the conflict as long as no one needs protection.

I follow up this lesson by informing all staff of the topics covered and encouraging them to reinforce the concepts when real conflicts arise by asking students, "Have you done anything to make the situation worse?" and "What could you do to make the situation better?"

This impromptu lesson is different from many of the other guidance lessons I have taught in that my role was purely one of investigation and facilitation. Studying what the students observed during the acute crisis yielded all the information needed. The young people analyzed the situation themselves, found solutions through discussion, and used those solutions to defuse the conflict within a day after the class discussions. Some of the students went on to make a video for the rest of the student body about what to do when friends fight. Those students presented their video at a Peace Day assembly the next fall.

When we enlist students in observing, analyzing, and creating solutions to class-wide or even school-wide problems, we give them the tools and confidence they will need to solve such problems throughout their lives. When students teach us about their world, both we and they benefit.

Recess School: Teaching Skills to Reduce Student Aggression

In 2000, the Bean school physical education teacher, Janet Hutchinson, came to me with an observation and an idea. She pointed out that some kindergarten and first-grade students were getting in trouble on the playground for hitting, pushing, and rough play. Having observed these same students in her physical education class, she could see that many of them had little sense of where their bodies were in regard to others' personal space. They seemed to possess only one speed of movement, fast and careless, and possessed limited skills in taking turns and playing games without fighting. Janet pointed out to me that unless these children learned the skills they were lacking, they would continue to lose recess time as a consequence for rough play. The less time they spent outside during recess, the less chance they would have to learn and practice the skills in which they were deficient. She proposed that we initiate a program to help students gain spatial awareness, regulate their activity level, learn to play without fighting, and take turns. When kindergarten and first-grade students lost recess time for rough play, we began to take them to the gym for what we called "recess school." Janet and I developed a set of fun games focused on teaching and providing opportunities to practice the desired skills.

Staff at the Bean school continue to teach and modify recess school. Over the years, we have found it most effective to implement recess school in a designated corner of the playground because this maximizes the likelihood that students will transfer the skills learned to regular, unstructured recess time. Recess school now runs during one 15-minute recess period each day. During the other recess block, all students attend recess together. When students in recess school lose recess time for aggressive behavior, we often allow them to return first to recess school and later to regular recess, but only when they show improvement in recess school. We assign students to recess school for an indefinite period of time, finding it more effective to keep students in recess school until we see change instead of assigning students to recess school for fixed time periods. We allow other students to wander into and participate in recess school, thus reducing stigma, encouraging positive peer role-modeling, and providing positive attention from adults for any student who desires it. When games become too large to supervise, we sometimes have to close recess school to some of these drop-in students. Since recess school is fun, students sometimes choose to continue to attend even after they are ready to graduate. We encourage them to stay if they so choose because we have found that young people who are removed from recess school sometimes choose to get in trouble again in order to rejoin.

In its present incarnation, recess school consists of three games and short discussions at the beginning and at the end. Before going outside to play, staff ask students to state the goals of recess school. Typical goals are to learn to play without hitting, be careful with their bodies, be gentle instead of rough, and calm down when they get mad. We review a few basic expectations. We then walk to our designated section of the playground and begin with a game Janet and I invented in 2000, which we call the Run and Don't Bump game. In this game, children are directed to run toward each other and to come as close as they can without bumping into each other. Most of the time students are very careful about following these rules, trying to see how close they can get without creating collisions. Rarely do they bump into each other. When they do bump, unless we see a clear intent to hurt, we help them jump right back into the game. We have found that this game teaches spatial awareness and helps students to scan their visual field to avoid colliding with peers while running. As I observe recess school graduates at play, I notice their newfound ability to run across the playground without knocking other children down.

The second game we play during recess school is the popular children's game Duck, Duck, Goose. To avoid boredom with daily play, we encourage students to change the words to *pizza, pizza, meatball; rabbit, rabbit, wolf;* or any other words students think of. After experimenting with many children's games, we have found that Duck, Duck, Goose provides an interesting level of challenge without too much competition, frantic running balanced by waiting, and simple rules. These elements of the game teach students to be patient, tag gently, run in a pattern, and make sure everyone gets a turn. As an added benefit, we have found that young people rarely grow tired of this game.

The third game we play with students during recess school is a modified form of Freeze Tag. In common versions of this popular game, one student is "It" until he or she "freezes" all the other students by tagging them. Since students who aren't It can "unfreeze" other players by tagging them, it can take a long time for a slower student to immobilize all the students playing. Because of this, slower students sometimes choose not to be It and withdraw from the game. Other students may become impatient and hit or push instead of playing the game fairly. To avoid the frustration caused by speed differences between students, in our version of Freeze Tag an adult calls out the name of a different child to be It about every 15 seconds. Our adaptation of the game helps children learn to tag gently, avoid collisions, and be flexible during situations that involve constant change. They also learn to wait their turn, and more athletic children learn to deal with not always being It.

At the end of recess school, the adult identifies one positive behavior exhibited by each student before sending the students back to their classrooms. Often we ask peers to identify a positive action exhibited by each student as well.

Staff play three main roles during recess school: They clarify the rules to reduce fights and cheating, enforce brief time-outs for aggressive behavior, and shower students with specific praise (e.g., "You tagged gently," "You waited your turn," "You used words," "You didn't bump anyone"). We have found recess school effective in reducing aggressive behavior and rough play.

Appendix E

Diversity in America: Using a True Story to Increase Motivation for Bystander Action

We developed the sessions next described after hearing an episode of the radio program *This American Life* titled "Shouting across the Divide" (Glass, 2006). This moving episode tells the true story of a well-liked Muslim student in a small-town elementary school in the United States. The Muslim student's classmates begin to harass her after her school distributes and teaches from an explicitly anti-Muslim book commemorating the 9/11 attacks. The story describes the inaction of other students, teachers, school board members, and community members. The lessons we developed incorporate excerpts from the radio story with discussion and a simulated reenactment of the girl's story. The radio program itself may be downloaded free or purchased on CD at www.thisamericanlife.org. Even if you do not plan to implement these lessons, I recommend that you listen to the radio program. The procedures described here could easily be adapted to provide a structure for creating a teaching simulation from a news story, movie, or book.

The story told in this radio program parallels in a more realistic and contemporary way the theme of Eleanor Estes's book *The Hundred Dresses* (2004/1944). In both stories, bystanders fail to act, and individuals are unfairly targeted, teased, and excluded because of some perceived difference between them and their classmates. The story also parallels the experiences of African Americans during the time of segregation, Jews during the Holocaust, and many other groups who have experienced discrimination throughout history and in the present day. The story addresses issues of cultural diversity and tolerance that are crucial to our students' ability to be successful, responsible citizens in an increasingly multicultural nation and interconnected world.

Students often relate well to the story, given that it is told primarily by an elementary school student and is set in the familiar setting of a modern-day American school. In addition, because the story is nonviolent, it does not lead to desensitization to violence. These lessons help students think about how they can be good citizens in a diverse country. Students have the opportunity to discover how many different individuals can work to solve problems of intolerance and exclusion in age-appropriate ways. The lessons also address a number of principles from our state's learning standards, which declare that each student must leave school a creative and practical problem solver and a responsible and involved citizen.

These sessions were scheduled for five or six 45-minute class sessions with fifth graders, although one could also adapt them effectively for work with adolescents or staff. I have found the sessions moving and effective for both students and teachers.

We begin each session with a greeting and a review of the previous session and end each class by keeping a project diary, included on page 178.

SESSION 1

During the first session, we define *diversity* and discuss the different types of diversity found in our town, state or region, and country. This first discussion should be tailored to meet the needs of each school and community. I often start with the following activity, inspired by a diversity lesson from Trudi Pinnick Wolfe called "What Can We Learn from a Box of Crayons?" (n.d.). The teacher or counselor empties and repacks boxes of crayons so that each box is full of crayons of only one color. Students are given paper with the boxes of crayons and asked to draw the most interesting pictures they can, using only the crayons given to them. When students complain about being limited to one color, we ask them how this exercise relates to discussions about diversity. We reinforce the idea that crayons, like people, are all different, but that it is the differences that allow us to make beautiful and interesting pictures. We end the first session by having students write answers to and then discuss the questions found in Worksheet 1, included on page 180.

We play the segments of the radio program indicated by the time codes during each of the following three sessions. Before playing the first segment—and for the duration of the remaining lessons—we randomly assign students to enact the following roles: three school board members, the main classroom teacher, three other school staff members, the principal, the Muslim student (two students share this role), the Muslim student's best friend, three other peers, the Muslim student's parents, and three other parents. We hand out the list of role descriptions on page 179 to help students start to think about their characters' positive goals.

Discussing each character's positive goals is often the most difficult aspect of this lesson. Many characters act on good intentions (i.e., a wish to be safe or keep others safe) in ways that impact others negatively. Through these discussions, students learn to place importance not just on intentions, but also on actions. They learn how to reach positive goals in ways that do not do harm.

While students listen to the radio story, we instruct them to pay particular attention to what their character does or fails to do that makes the situation better or worse. After listening to each segment, we provide time for students to voice their questions, thoughts, and emotional reactions. Some students at our remote rural school did not know what the word *Muslim* meant; students in any school will have strong emotional reactions to hearing the voice of a peer describe harassment.

Students then write about and discuss their characters' motivations, actions, and other choices. In all three audio excerpts, some characters' actions are clearly stated, while others' are omitted. When students do not hear their characters' actions described, we ask them to imagine what their characters might have done, based on the information they have about the story and about their characters' roles, listed on page 179. After they write, some students read their answers to the class, and we briefly discuss their answers. Worksheets for Sessions 2 through 5 are included on pages 180–184. We push students to focus on the nature of their roles, including the limitations their characters experience. When students strive for "right answers" or propose unlikely solutions, we should challenge them to question whether or not they would really use the proposed solution. Incorporating improvisational theater helps students test proposed solutions.

SESSION 2

The first excerpt from the radio program we play for students (Part 1: 7:28–14:36) includes an introduction to the Muslim student and her family and describes her family's decision to settle in a small town in the United States where few other Muslims live. We hear about the Muslim student's friendships and peer acceptance both before the 9/11 attacks and the year after.

SESSION 3

The third session focuses on another part of the story (Part 2: 14:15–21:51), which tells of the school system's decision to use a booklet that includes anti-Muslim statements to commemorate the first anniversary of the 9/11 attacks. This segment also explains how students changed their behavior toward the Muslim student and how her parents attempted to remedy the situation.

SESSION 4

During the fourth session, we listen to a segment of the radio program that describes the continued harassment of the Muslim student, which eventually leads her whole family to move to another community (Part 3: 21:15–38:50). This part of the story also identifies the effects of the harassment on the student, her family, and the school. Due to the length of this segment, you may wish to split this lesson into two parts.

SESSION 5

During the final session, we provide opportunities for students to review and apply the topics covered. To summarize the radio story and their characters' goals, actions, and potential actions, students fill out and discuss their answers to Worksheet 5, on page 184. To connect the series of lessons with wider issues, we review the pyramid of hate presented (Anti-defamation League, 2000) and identify examples of behaviors listed on the pyramid in the radio story. We also discuss parallels between the story and other historical or current incidents of injustice. We should encourage students to summarize and apply what they have learned by discussing how American citizens in a wide range of roles can act safely and effectively to prevent discrimination and exclusion. We can end by emphasizing that every person who is aware of bias, discrimination, or harassment can and should take a positive and helpful role to improve the situation—and by asking students to give examples of possible actions from the story and their own lives.

You may use or modify the worksheets on the following pages.

Project Diary

Date _____

What I learned in today's discussion:

_____

Date _____

What I learned in today's discussion:

_____

Date _____

What I learned in today's discussion:

_____

Date _____

What I learned in today's discussion:

_____

Date _____

What I learned in today's discussion:

Role Descriptions

Three school board members

School board members make decisions about what will be taught and which materials will be used. They choose the principal.

The classroom teacher

Teachers and other staff members work to help students learn and stay safe within the guidelines set by the school board and principal.

Three other school staff members—two teachers and an educational technician or paraprofessional

Teachers and other staff members work to help students learn and stay safe within the guidelines set by the school board and principal.

The principal

The principal supervises the teachers and tries to make the school a safe learning environment.

The Muslim student (two students share this role)

Young people want to have friends, have fun, and learn.

The Muslim student's best friend

Young people want to have friends, have fun, and learn.

Three other peers

Young people want to have friends, have fun, and learn.

The Muslim student's parents

Parents want children to be safe and happy and to live their lives the best they can.

Three other parents

Parents want children to be safe and happy and to live their lives the best they can.

Empowering Bystanders in Bullying Prevention: Grades K–8 © 2007 by Stan Davis. Champaign, IL: Research Press (800-519-2707; www.researchpress.com).

Worksheet 1: What Is Diversity?

What kinds of diversity are represented in this classroom?

In this grade?

In our school?

In our state?

In our country?

In what ways does diversity enrich our lives?

As you get older, in what ways will you have to be able to get along with and support the rights of others who are different from you?

Worksheet 2: Radio Story (Part 1)

What happened during this part of the story?

What did your character or group of characters do during this part of the story?

What positive goal was your character or group of characters trying to reach?

What were the results of your character's actions?

Worksheet 3: Radio Story (Part 2)

What happened during this part of the story?

What did your character or group of characters do during this part of the story?

What positive goal was your character or group of characters trying to achieve?

What were the results of your character's actions?

If the results were negative, what else could your character have done?

What would have been the results of this action?

What else could your character have done?

What would have been the results of this action?

Worksheet 4: Radio Story (Part 3)

What happened during this part of the story?

What did your character or group of characters do during this part of the story?

What positive goal was your character or group of characters trying to achieve?

What were the results of your character's actions?

If those results were negative, what else could your character have done?

What would have been the results of this action?

What else could your character have done?

What would have been the results of this action?

Worksheet 5: Summary

Who was your character?

What did your character do during the story?

What positive goals was your character trying to achieve?

What were the results of your character's actions?

If you were in the same role, what would you personally do?

What do you think would be the results of these actions?

What have you learned from this series of lessons?

Appendix F

Using Magic to Reinforce Positive Social Norms

Many of us in education bring our hobbies to work. School staff sing, cook, discuss local history, and build airplane models with their students as a way of sharing their own passions and thus making learning more personal, enjoyable, and memorable. Magic tricks are one such method of connecting with students and deepening learning.

Education based, group interventions to encourage inclusion, cooperation, and appreciation of diversity can be made more effective through the use of magic. I began learning magic effects in the 1990s after attending a workshop about using magic in counseling. Since then I have found magic to be a powerful tool to convey and reinforce messages to young people. Magic effects provide memorable visual reinforcement for a given topic and build a bond between students and adults. Several research studies also point to the effectiveness of magic. Lustig's (1994) study of magic focused on AIDS prevention and showed increased knowledge and self-efficacy when compared to a similar presentation lacking magic tricks. Spruill and Poidevant (1993) write, "Magic is an innovative and useful way of working with elementary students. It is action oriented, makes use of imagery and metaphor, is fun, and, most of all, involves the students." Rose (1998) and Arch (1993) describe the use of magic tricks to build connections and emphasize key points in presentations given to adults. In my own experience, magic can be used effectively with all age levels. I find that audiences not only react positively to presentations that include magic, they also gain a more durable and emotional understanding of concepts. Using magic builds our connections with students through shared enjoyment; communicates concepts vividly and viscerally; and makes learning intense, memorable, and participatory.

I began learning magic tricks to use in counseling to make connections with young people. As I deepened my interest in magic and studied with other magicians, read books, and watched instructional videos, I became aware of two equally important aspects of magic performance. First, there is the effect—the physical actions that confound expectations. Second, there is the presentation—the words, acting, and story that surround the effect. The presentation adds meaning to the effect.

Combining my interests in magic and theater, I have developed a series of presentations that use magic effects to convey messages about inclusion, bystander action, and other topics. Many of the materials required for the effects described here are commercially available. Learning magic tricks requires dedication and hours of practice and can be a source of great enjoyment. A good way to start is to find a local magician to take lessons from. There are also many good books for beginners, including Hay's (1982) *The Amateur Magician's Handbook,* Cassidy and Stroud's (1990) *The Klutz Book of Magic,* and Wilson's (2003) *Mark Wilson's Complete Course in Magic.*

The following pages describe a series of presentations using magic effects to convey messages. The presentations will describe what the audience sees and hears; the tricks themselves can be learned from directions that come with them or from books or videos. Some will require more practice than others.

With friendship, the more you give, the more you get.

The prop for this routine is called the Lota vase and is available from most magic shops and online. The Lota is a flower vase designed for magicians, that appears to refill itself with water repeatedly, even after being emptied. I start with a bouquet of flowers (real or plastic) in the Lota vase. I remove two flowers that look the same and say, "Sometimes we have friends who are just the same as us—people who like the same games, food, and music. This can be fun, but it can also be boring. I suggest finding friends who are different from you . . ." I remove several flowers that look different from the vase.

"Friends with different backgrounds and who have different interests." I point to the variety of flower shapes and colors in my hand and say, "That way life is less boring and more fun. Do you agree?" I ask students to tell me about someone quite different from them who turned out to be a good friend.

I continue: "We can make friends with all kinds of people because with friendship, the more you give, the more you get." I encourage students to repeat this phrase while I pour water from the vase into a nearby pitcher. I hold the vase upside down over the pitcher to show that the vase is empty.

I again prompt the audience to repeat the phrase "With friendship, the more you give, the more you get." While they say this, I pour more water out of the apparently empty vase. I prompt them again, and once more pour water out of the empty vase. I repeat this sequence: prompting students to repeat the friendship phrase while I pour more and more water out of the empty vase three or four more times during my workshop. The combination of repeated chanting and a magic effect help to cement this phrase in the minds of young people.

This presentation helps young people remember that reaching out to others will help them make interesting friendships.

Finding a good friend.

This presentation uses an effect called "The Super Dream Bag," which is commercially available from Denny and Lee Magic (www.dennymagic.com) and is based on a similar presentation by the magician Steve Taylor (n.d.). Easy to master, the effect allows one to remove objects from a paper bag previously shown to be empty. I begin the presentation with an ordinary-looking paper bag on the table in front of me. I state that in every school there are students who sit alone at lunch. I then remove an apple from my brown paper lunch bag. I say, "They sit alone because other people decide to exclude them, usually because of their outside characteristics." I gesture to the outside of the paper bag.

"Maybe they have different clothes, shoes, skin color, or hair. Those who choose to exclude them don't pay attention to their inside characteristics." I show the audience that the bag is empty inside.

I continue, "It's as if they don't have insides, only outside characteristics. But this is not a good way to choose friends, is it?" I ask the audience to brainstorm what makes a good friend, and I choose three characteristics from their ideas, such as kindness, sense of humor, and loyalty.

I go on to say, "When you get to know people who sit alone at lunch, you may find that they are kind . . ." As I say this, I remove a crystal box filled with paper flowers from the bag.

"Fun to be with . . ." I remove a second crystal box filled with flowers.

"And loyal." I remove a third crystal box from the bag.

"In fact," I add, "people who sit alone at lunch may be the best friends you will ever have." I attempt to fit the three boxes back into the bag and find that they fill it completely.

> *This presentation is helpful in moving students from feeling pity for other students who are excluded to seeing them as valued individuals. Students learn that including others benefits both others and themselves.*

When we help someone else, we make two people happy.

This presentation uses an effect called Bounce Across, created by the magician Daryl Martinez (www.foolerdoolers.com). Learning the sleight of hand involved in this effect requires some practice but is within the reach of a beginner who is willing to put in the effort. The effect involves a ball and a lump of clay. I begin the presentation by taking the ball out of my pocket and showing that it bounces. I ask, "If this ball were a person, what kind of person would it be?"

Students brainstorm and decide that bouncy people may be happy and excited to be alive and that they probably have friends to play with. I take the ball of clay out of my pocket and show that it does not bounce. I ask, "If this ball of clay were a person, what kind of person would it be?"

Students decide that the ball of clay may be lonely or sad and may not have any friends to play with. I bring two volunteers to the front of the room and hand one the ball and the other the clay. I ask the audience, "What can the happy ball do to help the sad clay feel better?"

Students often state that the ball can walk over to the clay and ask the clay to play. I prompt the student volunteers to act out this scene. The person holding the ball walks over to the person holding the clay, says, "Come play with me," and touches the ball to the clay. I then instruct the volunteer holding the ball to make sure it still bounces. We find that it does. I instruct the volunteer holding the clay to try to bounce the clay, and we find that now the clay bounces.

> *This presentation helps students see that asking others to play can make a big difference in their own and others' happiness.*

Whatever you do will be insignificant, but it is very important that you do it.

This routine, which I use to end most of my student and adult workshops, uses the commercially available effect Bubbles, Bubbles (www.magicfact.com). The effect allows a magician to blow bubbles into the air, pluck a bubble from the air, and show that it has transformed into a solid glass marble.

I begin the presentation by saying, "We have talked today about many things you can do when you see or hear bullying. Have you learned some new solutions to try when you are a bystander?"

After the audience answers yes (I would hope), I continue, "I want to leave you with a quote from Mahatma Gandhi, who reminded us not to let fear that our actions won't have a difference stop us from acting. You might worry that the solutions you have generated—such as helping targets get away from bullying, telling an adult, or sitting with a lonely peer at lunch— might not make a difference. Gandhi acknowledged this fear when he said, 'Whatever you do will be insignificant . . .' "

I blow bubbles from a bottle of bubble liquid I hold in my hand. I repeat, "Whatever you do will be insignificant . . ." as I blow more bubbles.

Again, I repeat, "Whatever you do will be insignificant . . ." and I blow a third stream of bubbles.

I pluck one of the bubbles from the air and finish the quote, "But it is very important that you do it." I gently knock the glass marble on the table, showing that it is solid.

I knock the marble on the table again. "But it is very important that you do it."

This presentation demonstrates that small effects can have large impacts.

Silence is consent.

This presentation is based on an effect described in Robert Neale's book *Tricks of the Imagination* (1991), designed to illustrate Niemöller's often quoted passage, written after the Holocaust (see p. 81). The effect will require some practice to master.

I begin by showing students photographs of three individuals. I tell the audience that I am about to read them a poem about three groups of people who were persecuted and killed during the Holocaust and about what happens when people are silent when they observe injustice. I begin to quote Niemöller:

"They came first for the Communists, and I didn't speak up because I wasn't a Communist." I show a photo to represent a communist and move that photo to the bottom of the pile of photographs I hold in my hand.

I continue, "Then they came for the Jews, and I didn't speak up because I wasn't a Jew." I show another photo to represent a Jew and move that photo to the bottom of the pile.

"Then they came for the trade unionists, and I didn't speak up because I wasn't a trade unionist." Again, I show a photo and move it to the bottom of the pile.

"Then they came for me, and by that time no one was left to speak up." As I say this, I show that all the photos in the pile are blank.

I show the first photo in the pile, now a blank piece of cardboard. I say, "Silence is consent," as I show the second photo to be blank as well.

I repeat, "Silence is consent," as I show the third photo, which now has a swastika on it.

This presentation helps students understand the urgency of acting while they can in the face of injustice, because at some point it will be too late.

What is bullying?

This routine uses the well-known magic effect called "The Professor's Nightmare" or "Equal-Unequal Ropes." Many magic books and videos teach the effect. My favorite method is taught in James Lewis's video *Million-Dollar Mysteries* (1992), easily found at many magic dealers'.

I begin with three ropes in my pocket—a long rope, a short rope, and a rope of medium length. I show the audience the long rope and say, "Young people who bully like to have a lot of power. They often enjoy and seek out the power to control and hurt others and decide who will have friends and who won't. They look around for someone to bully."

I swivel the top end of the rope as if it were a puppet. "They could bully someone who has friends and support," I say, as I take the medium-length rope out of my pocket.

"Or they could bully someone who has few friends and minimal support," I say, as I take the short rope out of my pocket.

I hold the three ropes in front of me, letting the ends dangle, and ask, "Who will the bully choose?" Students reply that the bully will choose a target with few friends and minimal support. When I ask why, they reply that it is easier to bully someone without support.

I drape the medium-length rope over my shoulder to get it out of the way. "When I was younger," I say, "adults told targets of bullying to solve the bullying problem themselves." I hold the long rope next to the short rope, which clearly shows the power imbalance between bullies and targets.

I ask, "What will bullies say if targets ask them to stop?" Students reply that bullies are likely to say no. They tell me that when targets use I-messages, such as "I feel hurt when you tease me," bullies are likely to say, "Good" or "So what?" I ask students why bullies are unlikely to change their behavior, and they reply that bullies enjoy their behavior and the feelings of power it provides. Thus the audience comes to realize that targets can't stop the bullying without help.

I say, "Until the rest of us intervene, the bully has a big smile," as I pick up the other end of the rope to make the shape of a smile.

"Bystanders are often happy as well," I say as I remove the medium-length rope from my shoulder and hold it in the shape of a smile.

"But targets are often sad," I say as I make the shape of a frown with the short rope.

I continue, "When we, as bystanders, find a safe way to help, . . ." I place the medium-length rope between the long rope and the short rope.

"We can take power away from the bully . . ." I begin to stretch the ropes so the long rope gets shorter and the short rope gets longer.

"And give power to the target." I continue to stretch the ropes so all three are the same length. I show each rope separately to reinforce that they are all the same length now. I smile at the audience and pause.

"Would you like to know the secret?" I ask. "Teamwork," I say after a pause, and I tie two of the ropes together, then tie them to the third, making one long rope.

"Teachers, parents, and bystanders can work together to make school a place where everyone belongs, everyone is safe, and where everyone comes to school with a big . . . ."

I hold the tied-together rope in the shape of a smile and wait for the audience to finish my sentence and say, "Smile."

This presentation helps students understand the unequal power dynamics involved in bullying, which in turn helps students develop and use safe and effective bystander solutions.

Beyond Elementary Schools

—Julia Davis

The principles discussed in this book and its predecessor, *Schools Where Everyone Belongs* (Davis, 2007), are widely applicable. While the principles and techniques described apply primarily within the context of public elementary schools, I clearly see the importance of the same concepts in our work with teenagers and in our lives as responsible citizens. This appendix will describe how I applied many of the core principles of effective bullying prevention programs to my work helping struggling teens gain the self-confidence and interpersonal skills needed to meet their goals effectively.

From March 2005 to July 2006, I worked for Summit Achievement in Stowe, Maine, a wilderness-based residential therapeutic treatment program for teenagers. Incorporating the principles of Reality Therapy, the program combines academics, wilderness expeditions, and therapy to help young people take responsibility for their behavior, make good choices, develop skills for interpersonal relationships, and set positive goals for the future. For eight days at a time, I lived with a team of five to nine students and two other staff members. I planned and facilitated expeditions, defused conflict, enforced rules, taught outdoor skills, and worked individually with students to help them set and achieve goals. I worked with therapists to develop and implement treatment plans.

We focused on encouraging students to take accountability for their behavior and recognize the consequences of their past and present behavior, empowering them to discover and practice more positive ways to meet their goals and helping them gain the confidence and motivation to create durable change. Given that the program is short term, we strove to inspire self-motivation for change instead of motivation arising from an attempt to please others. We encountered many challenges in working toward these goals. First of all, most students did not want to attend the program and thus were resistant to the program and staff. They were stuck in the limbo of adolescence—no longer children but lacking independence and control over their lives. They didn't want to be told what to do or think. Many saw no problem with their past actions and lacked motivation to change. Some possessed limited skills for interpersonal relationships or had become entrenched in patterns of behavior that were ineffective and often destructive. In order to help students succeed despite these challenges, we applied many of the principles and techniques described in this book. The three primary categories of overlap are as follows:

- Building staff-student connections through consistency, honesty, and choice of language.
- Helping students take accountability for their actions, realistically see the consequences of those actions, and meet their needs in more positive ways.
- Inspiring a peer environment of empathy and support.

Summit Achievement follows an ally-based counseling approach, emphasizing the importance of building staff-student connections to encourage change. Many of our students were at least initially resistant to trust or open up to program staff. Some had learned to see the adults in their lives as scapegoats or enemies. These initial attitudes often changed as students found that program staff did not judge them or put them down. Instead, we strove to listen to and validate students' thoughts and feelings; respect them as individuals; work with them to help them meet their goals; and work, learn, and play alongside them. We were consistent, fair, and honest and clearly expressed our expectations. In addition, given that direct care staff lived closely with students, we had the opportunity to get to know them and have fun with them during daily interactions. We frequently engaged in mutually enjoyable activities, met challenges side by side, and worked together toward common goals. As we have emphasized throughout this book, positive relationships with caring adults are an essential factor in helping young people consider and enact change. We strove to use the language of choices and consequences to help students take responsibility for past and present actions and to plan for future actions. We maintained positive feeling tone throughout our interactions with students, no matter what they did or said. When we stayed calm, students who acted out to inspire a negative reaction were not rewarded for their behavior, and those who focused their behavior solely on pleasing others could learn to set and work toward their own independent goals. In much of our work, we focused on asking open-ended questions and listening to and trying to understand students' thoughts and feelings. While open-ended questions have been presented thus far as a technique to help students develop, take ownership for, and implement effective and realistic solutions to social problems, they have another advantage in our work with teens. Open-ended questions show independent-minded youth that we value their opinions and don't see ourselves as having all the answers just because we are adults. As staff, we were better able to build positive relationships with students when we communicated consistent and clear expectations and consequences and followed through. Finally, we acted as positive role models by asking for and being willing to hear constructive feedback about our own behavior.

A second, and equally important, foundation of our work with teenagers was to help them meet their needs in more positive ways. One of the primary goals of the program was to help students acknowledge their past behaviors, take responsibility for the negative consequences of destructive behaviors, understand that other options exist, and develop skills and motivation to use alternative solutions in the future. As discussed in this book, all behaviors indicate a choice between options, and behavior problems are usually the result of misplaced attempts to meet positive goals. This aspect of our work strongly parallels chapter 3 of this book, on the topic of building empathy and social problem solving skills. The first step was to encourage students to be accountable for their behavior. The shock of being sent to a treatment program was often enough to cause students to take a look at their past actions. Through discussion with peers and adults within the context of a safe and accepting environment, many students were able to acknowledge their actions and recognize the consequences of these actions, both for themselves and for their families, friends, and teachers. Consistent rules, ensuring physical and emotional safety and clear expectations for students to move through the level system and thus graduate, gave staff the opportunity to reinforce cause-and-effect thinking and use the language of choices and consequences—thus clearly placing responsibility for change on the shoulders of students. When talking with students about their past behavior, I often used a modified version of the same four questions Stan uses when talking with aggressive youth about their behavior:

- What did you do?
- What was wrong with that?
- What goal were you trying to reach?
- The next time you have that goal, how will you reach it without hurting someone else?

I added to this discussion a focus not only on how students' actions affect others, but also on how their actions affect themselves. This focus was often effective with students who didn't care how their behavior impacted others. After helping students see the consequences of their past behavior and understand the goals they were trying to reach, we strove to help students develop more positive solutions. Skill development in this context was an everyday activity and relied on day-to-day interactions and conflicts with peers and staff as opportunities for practice. Given how closely we worked with students, we were able to pay attention to how they related to others and follow up frequently with them about the choices they were making, the consequences of those choices, and what other options were available. We acknowledged that changing behavior isn't easy and made sure not to expect immediate and drastic change.

We provided constant praise of the type described in chapter 2 of this book, on the topic of foundations for bullying prevention programs. Effective praise focuses students' attention on their own behavior and the positive consequences of that behavior. This type of praise, in combination with constructive feedback given with positive feeling tone, discourages students from blaming others for consequences and helps them continue positive behavior and change destructive behavior. We made it clear to students that they did not control our emotions. We communicated to them that they had the right to be proud of themselves when they did well and continued to work with them when they didn't succeed. We chose not to burden students with responsibility for our emotions. In this way, we helped them develop internal motivation for change. Another factor impacting the likelihood of behavior change is students' feelings of self-efficacy. By achieving success in the face of challenging situations—such as climbing a mountain or getting along with a diverse group of peers—students often developed faith in their ability to succeed. When students see their own strengths, they are also more likely to attempt change.

We followed Shure and Spivack's (1980, 1982) method of teaching problem-solving skills and empowering students to create their own solutions. This technique is especially helpful with defiant teenagers, who are often more resistant than younger students to adult direction and advice. We did not tell students what to do or not to do. Instead, we asked open-ended questions and provided space for students to reflect. Teenagers often possess a great deal of insight and understanding. When we listened to and valued this insight, we were able to ally with students and help them develop a range of solutions realistic for their temperament, home environment, and personal goals.

Group living was an important aspect of the program. Students lived with peers and staff and depended on one another for the basic necessities of life as well as for emotional support, entertainment, and insight. In order to facilitate a safe and supportive group environment, we employed many of the same techniques described throughout this book for achieving the goal of creating inclusive school communities. I have found adult role-modeling to be essential to this goal. When we model the skills involved in giving and receiving feedback, including and valuing all students, teaching and learning from one another, working together to achieve goals, and effectively dealing with our own physical and mental challenges, we help students develop these same skills. In addition, we enforced consistent guidelines for emotional and physical safety. Students were expected to be kind to and supportive of their peers, even if they didn't like them. Through nightly group meetings, we encouraged empathy and mutual understanding by requiring students, with feedback from the group, to share their past experiences and plan for the future. Every week, students received positive and constructive feedback from students and staff members. Through repeated practice, students learned to recognize positive actions in their peers as well as ways their peers could more effectively meet their goals. Students were required to teach other students who were new to the program essential knowledge and skills for wilderness travel. Through teaching, students connected with one another, and teachers further cemented their own skills and knowledge.

One of the reasons this book inspires me is the wide-ranging applicability I see for the core principles and techniques described. This is not a book just for elementary school staff. Many of the topics of this book are essential to working effectively with struggling teenagers. Specifically, our work with teens will be enhanced when we build staff-student connections, act as positive role models, focus on the language of choices and consequences, help students take accountability for their actions and build internal motivation for change, and inspire a peer environment of empathy and support. While we may change the details of our approach, the core values, goals, and strategies of this book can guide us in our work with people of all ages and from diverse backgrounds.

References and Bibliography

American Psychological Association (n.d.). Problem-solving program teaches kids how to use their heads instead of their fists. *Psychology Matters.* Retrieved January 25, 2007, from www.psychologymatters.org/shure.html

Anti-Defamation League. (2000). *A World of Difference® anti-bias study guide (Secondary level).* New York: Author.

Arch, D. (1993). *Tricks for trainers* (Vols. 1& 2). San Francisco: Jossey-Bass and Creative Training Techniques Press.

Aronson, E. (2000). *Nobody left to hate: Teaching compassion after Columbine.* New York: Owl Books.

Atlas, R., & Pepler, D. (1998). Observations of bullying in the class-room. *American Journal of Educational Research, 92*(2), 86–99.

Aveline, D. (2003). *Name calling, racial joking, and prejudice among students.* Bloomington, IN: Phi Delta Kappa Educational Foundation.

Benard, B. (1995). Fostering resilience in children. *ERIC Digest.* Retrieved February 13, 2007, from http://eric.ed.gov/ERICDocs/data/ericdocs2/content_storage_01/0000000b/80/2a/23/f8.pdf

Blacher, J., & Eisenhower, M. A. (2004). Overcoming peer rejection and promoting friendship. *Exceptional Parent Magazine.* Retrieved August 4, 2006, from www.eparent.com/researchreflections/researchreflections_2004_10.cfm

Bligh, D. A. (2000). *What's the use of lectures?* San Francisco: Jossey-Bass.

Bluestein, J. (2003). *What's wrong with I-messages?* Retrieved January 25, 2007, from www.janebluestein.com/articles/whatswrong.html

Branch, T. (1989). *Parting the waters: America in the King years, 1954–63.* New York: Simon and Schuster.

Branch, T. (1999). *Pillar of fire: America in the King years, 1963–65.* New York: Simon and Schuster.

Branch, T. (2006). *At Canaan's edge: America in the King years, 1965–68.* New York: Simon and Schuster.

Brendtro, L. K., Brokenleg, M., & Van Bockern, S. (1990). *Reclaiming youth at risk: Our hope for the future.* Bloomington: National Educational Service.

Brinkley, D. (2000). *Rosa Parks.* New York: Viking.

Brown, L. M. (2001). *Girlfighting: Betrayal, teasing and rejection among girls.* Retrieved January 28, 2007, from www.hardygirlshealthywomen.org/docs/girlfighting_paper.doc

Brown, L. M. (2005). *Girlfighting: Betrayal and rejection among girls.* New York: University Press.

Brown, L. M. (n.d.). *Creating safe, fair, and responsive schools.* Retrieved August 1, 2006, from www.stopbullyingnow.com/Brown_safe_schools.pdf

Buhs, E. S., Ladd, G. W., & Herald, S. L. (2006). Peer exclusion and victimization: Processes that mediate the relation between peer group rejection and children's classroom engagement and achievement? *Journal of Educational Psychology, 98*(1), 1–13.

Bunting, E. (1991). *A day's work.* New York: Clarion Books.

Bunting, E., & Himler, R. (1994). *Fly away home.* New York: Clarion Books.

Cassidy, J., & Stroud, M. (1990). *The Klutz book of magic.* Palo Alto: Klutz Press.

Chasnoff, D. [Director]. (2004). *Let's Get Real* [Video]. San Francisco, CA: Women's Educational Media.

City of Bothell, Washington. (n.d.). *Block watch program.* Retrieved August 12, 2006, from www.ci.bothell.wa.us/dept/PD/crimeprevention/blockwatch.html

City of Lawndale, California. (n.d.). *Neighborhood watch.* Retrieved August 4, 2006, from www.lawndalecity.org/html/depthtml/msd/neighbwatch.htm

Cohen, S. (producer), & Chasnoff, D. (director). (2003). *Let's get real* [Motion picture]. San Francisco: Women's Educational Media.

Cotton, K. (2001). Developing empathy in children. *Northwest Regional Educational Laboratory.* Retrieved November 24, 2006, from www.nwrel.org/scpd/sirs/7/cu13.html

Craig, W., & Pepler, D. (2000). *Making a difference in bullying* (LaMarsh Research Programme). Retrieved January 18, 2004, from www.yorku.ca/lamarsh/people/dpepler/art_01.html

Danish, S. J. (2000). Youth and community development: How after-school programming can make a difference. In S. J. Danish & T. Gullotta (Eds.), *Developing competent youth and strong communities through after-school programming* (pp. 275–301). Washington DC: Child Welfare League of America.

Danish, S. J., & D'Augelli, A. R. (1983). *Helping skills II: Life development intervention.* New York: Human Sciences.

Davis, S. (2007). *Schools where everyone belongs: Practical strategies for reducing bullying* (2nd ed.). Champaign, IL: Research Press.

Deci, E., & Flaste, R. (1996). *Why we do what we do: Understanding self-motivation.* New York: Penguin Books.

DiCamillo, K. (2000). *Because of Winn-Dixie.* Cambridge, MA: Candlewick Press.

Dweck, C. (2000). *Self-theories: Their role in motivation, personality, and development.* Philadelphia: Psychology Press.

Dweck, C. (2005). *Mindset: The new psychology of success.* New York: Random House.

Entenman, J. (2006). Rethinking the bystander role in school violence prevention. *Health Promotion Practice, 7*(1), 117–124.

Espelage, D. L., & Swearer, S. M. (2003). Research on school bullying and victimization: What have we learned and where do we go from here? *School Psychology Review, 32*(3), 365–383.

Estes, E. (2004). *The hundred dresses.* New York: Harcourt. (Original work published 1944)

Fekkes, M., Pijpers, F. I. M., & Verloove-Vanhorick, S. P. (2004). Bullying: Who does what, when and where? Involvement of children, teachers and parents in bullying behavior. *Health Education Research, 20*(1), 81–91.

Feshbach, N. D. (1983). Learning to care: A positive approach to child training and discipline. *Journal of Clinical Child Psychology, 12*(3), 266–271.

"From teasing to torment: School climate in America, a survey of students and teachers." (2005). New York: Harris Interactive and Gay, Lesbian, and Straight Network. Retrieved March 31, 2007, from: www.glsen.org/binary-data/GLSEN_ATTACHMENTS/file/499–1.pdf

Fuchs, D., Fuchs, L. S., Mathes, P. G., & Martinez, E. (2002). Social standing of students with learning disabilities in PALS and No-PALS classrooms. *Learning Disabilities Research and Practice, 14*(4), 205–215.

Garbarino, J., & DeLara, E. (2002). *And words can hurt forever.* New York: Free Press.

Garfield, J. (1957). *Follow my leader.* New York: Viking Press.

Gaughan, E., Cerio, J. D., & Myers, R. A. (2001). *Lethal violence in schools: A national survey.* Alfred, NY: Alfred University. Retrieved August 11, 2006, from www.alfred.edu/teenviolence/docs/lethal_violence_in_schools.pdf

Giovanni, N. (2005). *Rosa.* New York: Henry Holt.

Glass, I. (2006, December 15). *Shouting across the divide, episode 322* [Radio broadcast]. Chicago: This American Life (www.thisamericanlife.org).

Hanson, D. J. (n.d.). *Social norms marketing is highly effective.* Retrieved January 29, 2007, from www2.potsdam.edu/hansondj/YouthIssues/1093546144.html

Hay, H. (1982). *The amateur magician's handbook.* New York: New American Library.

Hazler, R. J. (2004). *Witnessing repeated abuse can affect bystanders.* Retrieved March 20, 2007 from www.alcoholism.about.com/od/abuse/a/blps041216.htm

Hekter, J. M., August, G. J., & Realmuto, G. M. (2003). Effects of pairing aggressive and nonaggressive children in strategic peer affiliation. *Journal of Abnormal Child Psychology, 31*(4), pp. 399–412.

Janson, G. R., & Hazler, R. J. (2004). Trauma reactions of bystanders and victims to repetitive abuse experiences. *Violence and Victims, 19*(2), 239–255.

Jeffrey, L. (2004). Bullying bystanders. *The Prevention Researcher, 11*(3), 7–8.

Jeffrey, L. R., Miller, D., & Linn, M. (2001). Middle school bullying as a context for the development of passive observers to the victimization of others. *Journal of Emotional Abuse, 2*(2/3), 143–156.

Jones, F. (2003). Dr. Fred Jones's tools for teaching: Weaning the helpless handraisers: Part 3. Teaching to the physical modality. *Education World.* Retrieved August 4, 2006, from www.education-world.com/a_curr/columnists/jones/jones005.shtml

Josephson Institute of Ethics. (n.d.). *Character counts: Children's books that build character.* Retrieved January 27, 2007, from www.charactercounts.org/booklist.php

Juvonen, J., Graham, S., & Schuster, M. A. (2003). Bullying among young adolescents: The strong, the weak, and the troubled. *Pediatrics, 112*(6), 1231–1237.

Katz, J. (2006). *The macho paradox: Why some men hurt women and how all men can help.* Naperville, IL: Sourcebooks.

Kimmel, M. S., & Mahler, M. (2003). Adolescent masculinity, homophobia, and violence: Random school shootings, 1982–2001. *American Behavioral Scientist, 46,* 1439–1458.

Kivel, P., & Creighton, A. (1997). *Making the peace: A 15-session violence prevention curriculum for young people.* Alameda: Hunter House.

Kluger, J. (2001). How to manage teen drinking (the smart way). *Time, 157*(24), 42–44.

Kohn, A. (1999). *Punished by rewards: The trouble with gold stars, incentive plans, A's, praise, and other bribes.* Boston: Houghton Mifflin.

Koppett, K. (2001). *Training to imagine.* Sterling, VA: Stylus Publishing.

Kuykendall, C. (2004). From rage to hope: Strategies for reclaiming Black and Hispanic students (2nd ed.). Bloomington, IN: National Educational Service.

Lee, E., Menkart, D., & Okazawa-Rey, M. (Eds.). (2002). *Beyond heroes and holidays: A practical guide to K–12 anti-racist, multicultural education and staff development* (2nd ed.). Washington, DC: Teaching for Change.

Lewis, J. (Producer). (1992). *Million-dollar mysteries: The magic of James Lewis.* [Motion picture]. (Available from www.frankelcostume.com/proddetail.php?prod=22–1943.)

Lodge, J., & Frydenberg, E. (2005). The role of peer bystanders in school bullying: Positive steps toward promoting peaceful schools. *Theory into Practice, 44*(4), 329–336.

Lowry, L. (1989). *Number the stars.* New York: Houghton Mifflin.

Ludwig, T. (2003). *My secret bully.* Portland, OR: Riverwood Press.

Ludwig, T. (2006). *Just kidding.* Berkeley: Tricycle Press.

Lustig, S. L. (1994). The AIDS prevention magic show: Avoiding the tragic with magic. *Public Health Reports, 109*(2), 162–167.

McCarthy, B. (1987). *The 4MAT system: Teaching to learning styles with right/left mode techniques.* Barrington, IL: Excel.

McCarthy, B. (2000). *About learning.* Wauconda, IL: About Learning.

McEvoy, A. (2005). *Teachers who bully students: Patterns and policy implications.* Philadelphia: Hamilton Fish Institute's Persistently Safe Schools Conference.

McGowan, M., McGowan, T., & Wheeler, P. (1994). *Appreciating diversity through children's literature: Teaching activities for the primary grades.* Englewood, CO: Teachers Ideas.

Montanaro, T. (1995). *Mime spoken here: The performer's portable workshop.* Gardiner, ME: Tilbury House.

Mullin, N. (2003). *Relational aggression and bullying: It's more than just a girl thing.* Wellesley Centers for Women: Wellesley, MA.

Mynard, H., Joseph, S., & Alexander, J. (2000). Peer victimization and post-traumatic stress in adolescence. *Personality and Individual Differences, 29,* 815–821.

Nansel, T. R., Overpeck, M., Pilla, R. S., Ruan, W. J., Simons-Morton, B., & Scheidt, P. (2001). Bullying behaviors among U.S. youth: Prevalence and association with psychosocial adjustment. *Journal of the American Medical Association, 285*(16), 2094–2100.

Neale, R. (1991). *Tricks of the imagination.* Seattle: Hermetic Press.

Newman, K. (2004). *Rampage: The social roots of school shootings.* New York: Basic Books.

Niemöller, M. (n.d.). *They came first for the communists.* Retrieved January 12, 2007, from www.nehm.org/contents/niemoller.html

Office of the New York State Attorney General Andrew M. Cuomo. (n.d.). *Neighborhood Watch: Learning the facts.* Retrieved August 6, 2006, from www.oag.state.ny.us/crime/neighborhood_watch/neighborhood_watch_toc.html

Olweus, D. (1993). *Bullying at school: What we know and what we can do.* Malden, MA: Blackwell Publishers.

Olweus, D. (1996). *The revised Olweus Bully/Victim Questionnaire.* Bergen, Norway: Hemil Center, Research Center for Health Promotion.

Olweus, D. (2001). *Olweus' core program against bullying and antisocial behavior: A teacher handbook.* Bergen, Norway: Hemil Center, Research Center for Health Promotion.

Olweus, D., Limber, S., & Mihalic, S. (1997). *Blueprints for violence prevention: Bullying prevention program.* Denver: C and M Press.

O'Neill, D. L., & Glass, B. A. (2000). *Kelso's choice: Conflict management skills.* Elgin, IL: Sunburst.

Ophelia Project. (n.d.). *Creating safe school climates.* Retrieved January 4, 2007, from www.opheliaproject.org/main/cass.htm

Paterson, K. (1978). *Bridge to Terabithia.* New York: HarperTrophy.

Paterson, K. (1979). *The great Gilly Hopkins.* New York: HarperTrophy.

Payne, R. (2001). *A framework for understanding poverty.* Highlands, TX: Aha! Press.

Pepler, D., & Craig, W. (2001). *Making a difference in bullying.* Retrieved January 27, 2007, from psyc.queensu.ca/~craigw/makediff.pdf

Pipher, M. (2002). *The middle of everywhere.* New York: Harcourt.

Ranson, J. F. (2005). *Don't squeal unless it's a big deal: A tale of tattletales.* Washington DC: Magination Press.

Rappaport, D. (2001). *Martin's big words: The life of Dr. Martin Luther King, Jr.* New York: Hyperion Books for Children.

Rigby, K. (n.d.). *Do interventions to reduce bullying in a school really work?* Retrieved February 12, 2007 from www.education.unisa.edu.au/bullying/intervention.htm

Rigby, K., & Slee, P. T. (1991). Bullying among Australian school culture: Reported behaviour and attitudes to victims. *Journal of Social Psychology, 131,* 615–627.

Rose, E. (1998). *Presenting and training with magic: 53 simple magic tricks you can use to energize any audience.* New York: McGraw-Hill.

Ross, D. (2003). *Childhood bullying and teasing* (2nd ed.). Alexandria, VA: ACA Press.

Russell, S. T., McGuire, J. K., Laub, C., Manke, E., O'Shaughnessy, M., Heck, K., & Calhoun, C. (2006). *Harassment in school based on actual or perceived sexual orientation: Prevalence and consequences* (California Safe Schools Coalition Research Brief No. 2). San Francisco: California Safe Schools Coalition.

Salmivalli, C., Lagerspetz, K., Bjorkqvist, K., Osterman, K., & Kaukiainen, A. (1996). Bullying as a group process: Participant roles in their relations to social status within the group. *Aggressive Behavior, 22*(1), 1–15.

Salmivalli, C., & Voeten, M. (2004). Connections between attitudes, group norms, and behaviors associated with bullying in schools. *International Journal of Behavioral Development, 28,* 246–258.

Sanford, L. (1992). *Strong at the broken places.* New York: Avon.

Saufler, C. (2006). *Homophobic bullying and the 10-second intervention.* Retrieved August 10, 2006, from www.stopbullyingnow.com/tensecondintervention.pdf

Scottish Executive. (1999). *Let's stop bullying: Advice for young people.* Retrieved January 27, 2007, from www.scotland.gov.uk/library2/doc04/lsby-00.htm

Sharp, S., & Smith, P. (Eds). (1994). *Tackling bullying in your schools.* New York: Routledge.

Shure, M. B. (1995). Teach your child how, not what, to think: A cognitive approach to behavior. *Brown University Child and Adolescent Behavior Letter, 11*(8), 5–6.

Shure, M. B. (1996). *Raising a thinking child: Help your young child learn to resolve everyday conflicts and get along with others.* New York: Pocket Books.

Shure, M. B. (2000). *Raising a thinking child workbook: Teaching young children how to resolve everyday conflicts and get along with others.* Champaign, IL: Research Press.

Shure, M. B. (2001a). *I Can Problem Solve (ICPS): An interpersonal cognitive problem-solving program—Preschool.* Champaign, IL: Research Press.

Shure, M. B. (2001b). *I Can Problem Solve (ICPS): An interpersonal cognitive problem-solving program—Kindergarten and primary grades.* Champaign, IL: Research Press.

Shure, M. B. (2001c). *I Can Problem Solve (ICPS): An interpersonal cognitive problem-solving program—Intermediate elementary grades.* Champaign, IL: Research Press.

Shure (2006). *A problem solving approach to prevention of high-risk behaviors from the preschool through the middle-school years.* Retrieved January 2007 from http://hamfish.org/conference/2006/Proceedings/636%20A%20problem%20solving%20approach%20to%20prevention%20of%20high-risk%20behaviors.pdf

Shure, M. B., & Spivack, G. (1980). Interpersonal problem solving as a mediator of behavioral adjustment in preschool and kindergarten children. *Journal of Applied Developmental Psychology, 1,* 29–44.

Shure, M. B., & Spivack, G. (1982). Interpersonal problem-solving in young children: A cognitive approach to prevention. *American Journal of Community Psychology, 10,* 341–356.

Singh, M. (1998). *Gender issues in children's literature.* Retrieved January 27, 2007, from www.indiana.edu/~reading/ieo/digests/d135.html

Smith, P. K., & Shu, S. (2000). What good schools can do about bullying. *Childhood, 7*(2), 193–212.

Spruill, D. A., & Poidevant, J. M. (1993). Magic and the school counselor. *Elementary School Guidance and Counseling, 27*(3), 228–233.

Stein, N. (1999). *Classrooms and courtrooms: Facing sexual harassment in K–12 schools.* New York: Columbia University Teachers College Press.

Stein, N., & Cappello, D. (1999). *Gender violence, gender justice.* Wellesley, MA: Wellesley College Center for Research on Women.

Stein, N., & Sjostron, L. (1994). *Flirting or hurting? A teacher's guide on student-to-student sexual harassment in schools for grades 6–12.* Wellesley, MA: Wellesley College Center for Research on Women.

Stueve, A., Dash, K., O'Donnell, L., Tehranifar, P., Wilson-Simmons, R., Slaby, R. G., & Link, B. G. (2006). Rethinking the bystander role in school violence prevention. *Health Promotion Practice, 7*(1), 117–124.

Sugai, G., Sprague, J. R., Horner, R. H., & Walker, H. M. (2000). Preventing school violence: The use of office discipline referrals to assess and monitor school–wide discipline interventions. *Journal of Emotional and Behavioral Disorders, 8*(2), 94–101.

Taylor, S. (n.d.). *Educational magic.* Retrieved February 18, 2007, from www.stevetaylorpro.com/educational.htm

Teicher, S. A. (2006). "Social norms" strategy aims to tame bullying. *Christian Science Monitor, 98*(184). Retrieved January 27, 2007, from www.csmonitor.com/2006/0817/p15s02-legn.html

Thorne, B. (1993). *Gender play: Girls and boys in school.* New Brunswick, NJ: Rutgers University Press.

University of Melbourne. (2006). Teens who "bite back"' risk bullying—study. *UniNews, 15*(23), 11–25. Retrieved January 12, 2007, from uninews.unimelb.edu.au/unarticleid_3929.html

Upright, R. L. (2002). To tell a tale: The use of moral dilemmas to increase empathy in the elementary school child. *Early Childhood Education Journal, 30*(1), 15–20.

Vaillancourt, T., Hymel, S., & McDougall, P. (2003). Bullying is power: Implications for school-based intervention strategies. *Journal of Applied School Psychology, 19,* 157–176.

"Welcome to Persona Doll Training!" (n.d.). Retrieved January 27, 2007, from www.persona-doll-training.org

Wellman, S. (2002). Reducing relational aggression. *The Fourth and Fifth Rs: Respect and Responsibility Newsletter, 9*(1). Retrieved August 16, 2006, from www.catholiceducation.org/articles/parenting/pa0077.html

Wilson, M. (2003). *Mark Wilson's complete course in magic.* Philadelphia: Running Press.

Wolfe, T. P. (n.d.). *What can we learn from a box of crayons?* Retrieved February 16, 2007, from www.tolerance.org/teach/activities/activity.jsp?ar=691

Young, E. (2006). Relational aggression: Understanding, identifying, and responding in schools. *Psychology in the Schools, 43*(3), 297–312.

About the Authors

Stan Davis began working for human rights in the 1960s during the civil rights movement. Starting in the late 1960s, he worked as a child and family therapist in residential treatment, community mental health, and private practice. During his years as a therapist, he was active in building positive community support for targets of child abuse, rape, and domestic abuse. Stan became a school guidance counselor in the mid-1980s and began to focus on bullying prevention in the late 1990s. He currently works part-time at the James H. Bean Elementary School in Sidney, Maine. Stan also trains educators, parents, and students nationwide in effective bullying prevention. He is a certified Olweus bullying prevention consultant and a founding member of the International Bullying Prevention Association.

The Bean school's bullying prevention program, which has shown dramatic reductions in student reports of bullying, and Stan's nationwide trainings have been the subject of newspaper, magazine, and TV stories, including a *20/20* report by ABC's John Stossel. His first book, *Schools Where Everyone Belongs: Practical Strategies for Reducing Bullying,* was published by Research Press in 2005, with a second edition published in 2007. Stan also maintains www.stopbullyingnow.com, an informative Web site for concerned parents and educators.

Julia Davis, Stan's daughter and coauthor, has lent clarity to Stan's writing about bullying prevention since 2003. She brings to the table her own experiences working with young people of all ages and from diverse backgrounds. She began working with young people in 1999 and has since led high school trail crews for the Student Conservation Association, developed and taught experiential natural history lessons, taught English in an underprivileged elementary school in Costa Rica, and led outdoor expeditions for Summit Achievement, a wilderness-based therapeutic treatment center for teens. In her work with young people, Julia often implements adapted versions of the principles described in this book and its predecessor, *Schools Where Everyone Belongs.*

Julia's interest in writing and editing arose while she attended College of the Atlantic, where she worked as a writing tutor and teaching assistant for an introductory writing class and wrote a series of nature essays for her senior project. In addition to pursuing freelance writing and editing (www.editingforclarity.com), she plans to study documentary writing at the Salt Institute for Documentary Studies in Portland, Maine.

Empowering Bystanders DVD

This DVD features a 50-minute audiovisual presentation. In it, author Stan Davis provides an extensive discussion, accompanied by PowerPoint slides, to help illustrate and expand upon important ideas covered in the book.

During the presentation, he provides a detailed overview of the program, cites bullying research, offers suggestions and implementation guidelines, and includes numerous personal observations.

The DVD can be used for individual learning, book study groups, or staff inservice training.

An 18-page PDF file with duplicates of the slides in the presentation as well as room for taking lecture notes is available at www.stopbullyingnow.com/empoweringbystanders.pdf.